抗戰的中共

林邁可

By the same author.

Educational Problems in Communist China. New York, Institute of Pacific Relations, 1950.

The New China: Three Views. With Otto van der Sprenkel and Robert Guillaine. London, Turnstile Press, 1950.

China and the Cold War. Melbourne University Press, 1955.

Is Peaceful Co-existence Possible? Michigan State University Press, 1960.

Section on "History and Doctrines of the Chinese Communist Party" in **China: A Handbook**, edited by Yuan-li Wu. New York, Praeger, 1973.

The Unknown War
North China 1937-1945

Michael Lindsay

Professor Emeritus of Far Eastern Studies, The American University, Washington D.C.

Bergström & Boyle Books Limited, London. 1975

Produced and published by Bergström & Boyle Books Limited
22 Maddox Street London W1R 9PG

© Michael Lindsay 1975

Designed by Tamasin Cole & Theo Bergström

Bromides by John Couzins

Printed in Great Britain by
Butler & Tanner Ltd The Selwood Printing Works
Frome Somerset BA11 1NF

Bound by
J. M. Dent & Sons Ltd The Aldine Press
Letchworth Herts SG6 1LF

ISBN 0 903767 05 8

The war against Japan in North China remained almost unknown to the outside world from 1938 to 1944. This book contains the only photographic record by a foreign observer who worked in the Chinese Communist organisation during this period.

Central Hopei landscape.

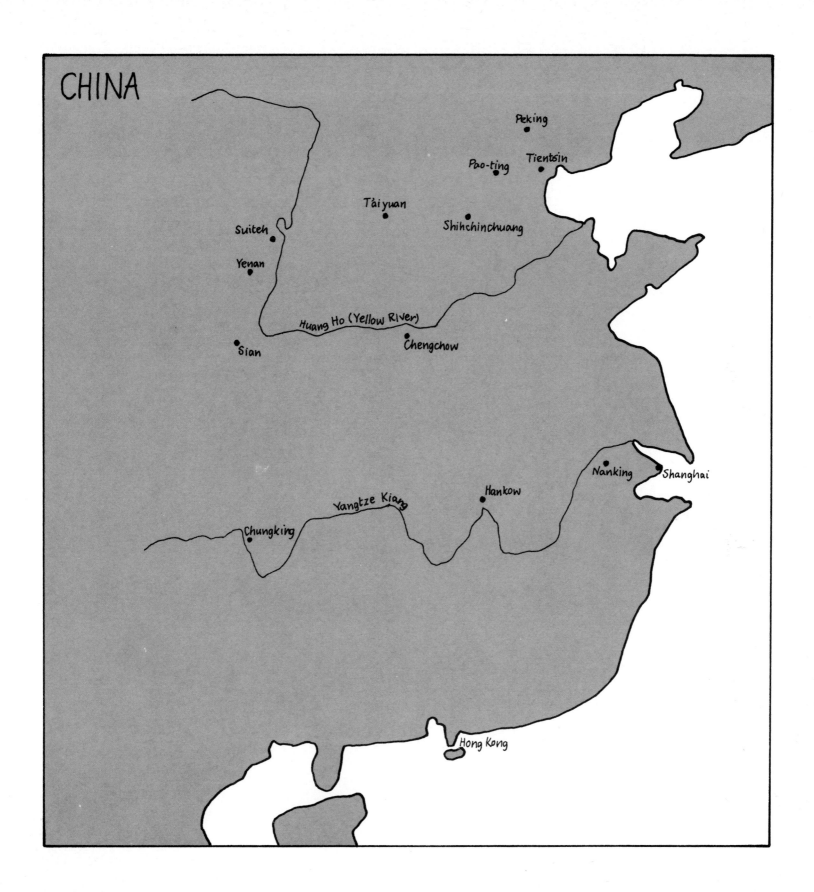

Introduction

Old city of Yenan.

A number of writers have suggested that Mao Tse-tung has a nostalgia for the period he spent at Yenan. This would not be unreasonable because the Chinese Communists were most successful during this period, and it could truthfully be called the heroic age of Chinese Communism. They started in 1937 controlling an area with a population of about a million and with an army of about thirty thousand. By the time of the Japanese surrender in 1945 they controlled areas with a population of nearer one hundred million and had an army of nine hundred thousand.

A lot has been written about Yenan and its surrounding country, the Shensi-Kansu-Ninghsia Border Region, and one still sometimes finds reference to Northwest China as the area the Communists controlled during the war with Japan. While Shensi-Kansu-Ninghsia could be described as northwest, the Communist expansion during the war was entirely eastwards and southwards, and already by the summer of 1938 several of the new Communist base areas had larger populations than Shensi-Kansu-Ninghsia. In the spring of 1945 I tried to work out the centre of population of Communist controlled territory and estimated that it was in southern Hopei or western Shantung, some five hundred miles east-south-east of Yenan. Leaving out Manchuria, it would be more correct to refer to the areas under Communist control as Northeast China.

The Yenan area was important because the Japanese never penetrated west of the Yellow River. Shensi-Kansu-Ninghsia, therefore, suffered no damage from the war, except for the bombing of the old city of Yenan in early 1938, while the other Communist regions were frequently fought over and a large proportion of their towns and villages destroyed by the Japanese. Yenan was, therefore, a convenient centre for headquarters organisations. However, for the war time Communist areas as a whole, Yenan and Shensi-Kansu-Ninghsia were something like the District of Columbia or the Australian Capital Territory; important only as the location of the central organisation.

Most of my travels were in Chin-Ch'a-Chi (Shansi-Ch'ahar-Hopei) which was one of the largest Communist areas with a population of around twenty five million. Also, the earliest war time base to be organised, it was unique in receiving recognition from the National Government as a special war time authority equivalent to a provincial government. Up to late 1943 it had an openly functioning Kuomintang party organisation and the civilian government included several Kuomintang members. Its organisation and development are discussed in a forthcoming book by Karl A. Dorris (University of California Press) who shows that a number of important war time Communist policies originated there.

Chin-Ch'a-Chi government Headquarters, Wu-t'ai area.

Sung Shao-wen, chairman of Chin-Ch'a-Chi government with assistant, Wu-t'ai.

Hu Jen-k'uei, finance minister and Kuomintang representative in Chin-Ch'a-Chi government.

Under war time conditions, the natural boundaries for any Chinese controlled area in North China were the Japanese held railways. Mountain ranges, natural boundaries in peace time, became natural base areas for anti-Japanese organisations.

Most of Chin-Ch'a-Chi was bounded by railways: on the north by the Peking — Tat'ung, on the east by the Peking — Shih-chia-chuang, in the south by the Shih-chia-chuang — T'aiyuan, and on the west by the T'aiyuan — Tat'ung. Much of this was very wild mountain country with almost no roads. In the one hundred and eighty miles between the Peking — Tat'ung and the Shih-chia-chuang — T'aiyuan railways, only one road crossed the ranges and it, like most roads in North China at that time, was little more than a strip of land reserved for traffic over which one could drive a small lorry with good ground clearance. Mule or oxen carts were more common, and the rougher mountainous areas had no roads at all, goods could only be moved by pack animals or porters. On the trip through there in 1939 we travelled for some two hundred miles without seeing a single wheeled vehicle.

Chin-Ch'a-Chi also included Central Hopei, east of the Peking—Hankow railway, an almost flat plain, though for military purposes it allowed some cover from the varying levels between fields, from sunken roads, and during the summer from tall crops, especially *kao-liang*—a variety of sorghum which grew about ten feet high. Central Hopei was far more prosperous and economically developed than the mountain areas—it was the major cotton growing area in China and a mechanized textile industry had developed in some of the cities. Once the Japanese began a serious effort to control the North China countryside at the end of 1938, they soon captured all the towns but, except for a

short period in 1942, the Communist forces retained control of a great deal of the countryside. In August 1942 the Japanese staged a major offensive there and forced the regular Communist troops to retire to the mountains west of the Peking-Hankow railway. In 1961 in Tokyo I met a former officer from the North China Army Headquarters who knew from his own experience that in September 1942 a Japanese officer could travel unescorted in Central Hopei. However, the Japanese did not destroy the Communist organisation though General Lü Cheng-ts'ao told me that he had lost almost a third of his local officials. When Japanese pressure relaxed in early 1943 Communist troops began moving back and by 1945 members of the U.S. Army Observers Section from Yenan were able to visit Central Hopei.

Chin-Ch'a-Chi also included land along the Hopei-Jehol-Liaoning border, though this was not a regular base area. East Hopei, north of the Peking-Tientsin railway, had come under effective Japanese control in 1935 as the East Hopei Autonomous Area. In July 1938 the entry of some Communist troops touched off a general revolt and for a few weeks the Japanese lost control. This was a vital strategic area, astride their communications from Manchuria, and they sent in large numbers of troops to supress the revolt and then established very tight controls making it hard for a new resistance movement to develop. I met one man who had worked there who said that one could not even settle down to kill off the lice in ones clothes because police raids on the villages, with inspections of residents' permits to catch infiltrators, came so frequently and so suddenly.

Southeast Shansi was another Communist base area in wild mountain country and, until 1941, the main Eighteenth Group Army Headquarters of Generals Chu Te and P'eng Te-huai was there and not at Yenan. South Shansi, a less mountainous area with larger towns, was, until 1943, held by National Government troops and not by Communists.

During the 1930's the Chinese National Government was steadily improving its regular army and wanted, therefore, to postpone a full scale war with Japan for as long as possible. From the purely military point of view, this was a sensible policy; politically it was more doubtful. The Chinese government could not explain its policy to the people because this would have been an invitation to the Japanese army to grab everything it wanted in China while the going was good. The Chinese public saw their government meeting a series of Japanese encroachments with compromises and concessions and became more and more dissatisfied. July 7th. 1937 is the accepted date for the start of the Sino-Japanese war but for more than a month fighting was confined to the Peking-Tientsin area while negotiations went on between the Chinese and Japanese governments.

The Japanese army leaders would have been pleased to settle the fighting of July 1937 as a local incident if they could have got further concessions to strengthen their position in North China, but Chiang Kai-shek could not afford to concede more. Lo Chia-lun, an old and very loyal member of the Kuomintang, once described to me his fears that there would be further concessions at this date and his relief on hearing from a member of Chiang Kai-shek's secretariat that Chiang had decided to send eight divisions into Hopei. Since this was contrary to the terms of an earlier agreement with Japan it showed that the Chinese government had finally decided to fight.

When in late August the fighting began to spread the Japanese not only advanced rapidly in the North China plain but also broke through the passes into Shansi. There was fighting in Shanghai where the National Government troops, well trained and equipped, held the Japanese until they were outflanked by a landing in Hangchow Bay.

By the beginning of 1938 the Japanese had defeated the regular Chinese armies north of the Yellow River but until October 1938 they made little serious attempt to control the countryside away from the railways. This gave the Communists their opportunity. Although the Long March from late 1934 to 1936 was a remarkable military exploit it belongs in the same class as Dunkirk in British history. It was remarkable that the Red Army managed to survive but while Communist forces in South and Central China had previously totalled about three hundred thousand, in 1937 even after local recruitment it only totalled some forty thousand—thirty thousand in the new northwest base area, and about ten thousand remnants in South China who became the New Fourth Army.

In 1936 when the Comintern line changed from "united front from below" to "united front from above" negotiations started between the Communists and the Kuomintang National Government, but it was only with the Sian Incident in December 1936 that the civil war effectively ended, and it was not until September 1937 that an agreement was reached between the National Government and the Communists under which the Communist forces in the northwest were recognised as the Eighth Route Army with three divisions, the 115th., the 120th. and the 129th. while the remnants in South China were recognised as the New Fourth Army with an original strength of about ten thousand. (Communist documents of the period show that the Party leadership was worried that the fighting from July 1937 would be settled as a local incident).

There is evidence of disagreement within the Communist leadership about military policy in the early period of the war. Leaders with close ties to the Soviet Union opposed guerilla warfare while others advocated it from the start. The chief of staff of one subdistrict in Chin-Ch'a-Chi told me that there had been discussions of a move into Manchuria. It was expected that the National Government armies would be able to hold the passes out of the North China plain for some time, and, if this had happened, the mountainous areas of Jehol and southern Liaoning would have been the only territory in North China suitable for guerilla warfare.

In fact, at the request of Yen Hsi-shan, the provincial warlord who had been made commander of the 2nd. War Zone, the Eighth Route Army moved across the Yellow River to assist in the defence of Shansi. The 115th. division inflicted a serious defeat on a Japanese force advancing southwards through the pass of P'ing-hsing-kuan but the Japanese captured the provincial capital, T'aiyuan, in November and continued their advance. This left the 115th. in northeast Shansi completely surrounded by Japanese held railways; the 129th. in southeast Shansi with Japanese held railways to the north, east and west; and the 120th. in northwest Shansi, across the Yellow River from the Yenan area.

With the Japanese only holding the railways, much of the countryside was a political vacuum. Many former local officials had left with the regular Chinese armies and numerous local anti-Japanese organisations had sprung up, some led by local gentry, some by officers left behind in the Chinese retreat, and others by local minor warlords or by various political activists. The Communists were able to provide a cadre of men with long experience of guerilla warfare against an enemy with far superior fire power and to offer the advantages of a larger organisation.

Under the united front agreement of September 1937 the Communists had promised to give up such specifically Communist policies as confiscation of land from landlords and to base themselves on Sun Yat-sen's principles. The resulting policies were, in fact, far more effective in winning general popular support than the purely Communist policies of the Chinese Soviet Republic. On the key issue of land reform, the Communists based their policy on a law that the National Government had issued in 1930, but did not effectively enforce until after its withdrawal to Taiwan in 1949, limiting rent to 37.5% of the main crop and giving the tenant considerable security without making the landlord's position intolerable.

A very important reform which took much longer to implement was in the taxation system. This had been both inefficient and inequitable; inefficient because a good deal of what was collected from the tax-payer did not reach the government, inequitable not only because many taxes were regressive but also because of widespread evasion. It was estimated that roughly a third of all land had, somehow, got off the registers for land tax which was a major source of revenue and, potentially, fairly equitable. (The Communist areas in Shantung retained land tax throughout the war.)

Quite apart from definite policies, the provision of honest government was vital in winning popular support. People at Yenching University said that, before the war, if a graduate had political connections and wished to get a graduate degree abroad, he would often take an appointment as *hsien-chang,* a position roughly equivalent to District Officer in the old British colonial system. On a nominal salary of a few hundred American dollars a year, he could save enough from a year's service to finance his study in the United States. When one graduate acting as *hsien-chang* actually tried to help the people of his district, the grateful population erected a memorial in his honour. It took some time to win real support from a population that was justifiably sceptical of promises from any government. It also took time to make efficient soldiers out of the various small anti-Japanese units and the mass of new recruits. The conditions through much of 1938 were almost ideal for such military training with a certain amount of light fighting in attacks on the Japanese held railways or countering the comparatively small Japanese raids into the countryside.

In October 1938 the Japanese finally began a definite attempt to gain control of the North China countryside but, by now, it had been organised against them and the Chinese troops were a serious fighting force. By the end of 1939 the Japanese had captured all the *Hsien* cities in Chin-Ch'a-Chi, excepting Fup'ing which was far into the mountains and had been reduced to ruins by a raid in 1938. However, they had not eliminated the Chinese forces which had actually become larger since 1938 and they had taken quite heavy losses. In one engagement a Japanese Lieutenant General was killed.

For the Japanese, the long delay in operations against the North China countryside was a major mistake. I was given an explanation for this in 1961 when talking with a group of officers in the History Section of the National Defence Force in Tokyo, officers who had served in North China and Manchuria. When asked about this delay they admitted that the Japanese army had staged the Mukden Incident in 1931, but insisted that the Luk'ouch'iao Incident in July 1937 was unexpected. They had not at this time prepared for a major war in China, and did not have sufficient troops ready. They had to choose between gaining control of the North China countryside and dealing with the regular armies of the National Government. Choosing the latter left only the 110th. division to guard all their lines of communication in the North and this explanation fits the evidence; after capturing Wuhan and Canton, their major objectives in Central and South China in September 1938, the Japanese transferred large numbers of troops to North China.

The Japanese also failed to maintain discipline, another major mistake. In the summer of 1938 an Eighth Route Army officer remarked to Professor George Taylor and me that it was difficult to develop anti-Japanese organisation in any place the Japanese had not been. Wherever they had been, the army record for looting, rape and indiscriminate killing was so bad that an anti-Japanese organisation could get full support from the local population. Someone at Yenan told me of an area in Shansi which had changed hands between Japanese, Kuomintang and Communists where the local saying was, "Japanese, too many killed; Kuomintang, too many taxes; Communists, too many meetings."

Certain Japanese officers realised the disastrous effects of bad discipline. In the fighting in western Hopei in 1939 the Communists captured a Japanese regimental headquarters. Among the documents they found was a report of a speech to his officers by General Kuwaki of the 110th. Division in which he stated that, unless the army could greatly improve its discipline towards the civilian population, Japan would lose the war in China. However, he was apparently unable to do anything about it. In my talks with officers in the History Section of the National Defence force, they tried to suggest that reports of Japanese atrocities were Communist propaganda. I made clear that this was contrary to the evidence and went on to say that the basic trouble seemed to have been that the Kempetai had got out of hand; somewhat to my surprise they all agreed. The Kempetai were both the military and the political police and an extremely powerful organisation which no ordinary officer could safely oppose. They were also extremely corrupt and deeply involved in the drug traffic and other forms of racketeering.

The declining standards of the Japanese army are an interesting subject. During the Russo-Japanese war it was highly praised by all foreign observers for its excellent discipline both towards, the civilian population and towards prisoners. By the 1930's and 1940's the Japanese army was notorious for its bad discipline in both these respects.

The falling standards are sometimes explained by the fact that the officer corps of the Russo-Japanese war came from samurai families with their tradition of discipline. This may in part be the explanation but the influence of two general principles could be more important. An organisation loses the power to control its least reputable members when solidarity and preserving the good name of the organisation are taken as the highest virtues. There is clear evidence that highly placed Japanese, including the emperor, did not care for the behaviour of the adventurers and fanatics, but they were never willing to challenge the argument that strong disciplinary action would discredit the army's good name. Again, when at Japanese army press conferences foreign correspondents in Peking brought up reports of atrocities the standard reply of army spokesmen was that they denied such reports on principle because such behaviour would be contrary to the Meiji rescript on army discipline.

In 1904-5 the Japanese army could feel with some justification that it was fighting to liberate Asia from Western imperialism. From the Siberian Expedition on, the objectives of the army leaders were not really defensible. No Japanese officer could retain his self respect if he thought clearly and compared the high sounding claims of the "new order in East Asia" with what the army was actually doing.

In the campaigns of 1939 the main Japanese move against the Communist forces was an encirclement strategy which the main units invariably evaded. In 1940 a new strategy began. It is said that General Kuwaki had studied the records of the National Government campaigns against the Chinese Soviet Republic in which the fort and blockade line strategy had finally forced the Communists to abandon their bases in South China and retreat in the Long March.

The system of forts and blockade lines, started as a means to protect the railways, was extended, gradually cutting down the Communist base areas. Continuing offensives into these areas no longer seriously tried to surround the main Communist forces but concentrated on maximum damage to areas not controlled by the fort and blockade line system. Villages were burned, farm animals killed, crops and food stores removed or destroyed, and captured civilians taken off for labour in Manchuria.

As in South China, the Communists had no fully effective counter. In August 1940 they attempted their own major counter-offensive, the Hundred Regiment Campaign, capturing many Japanese positions and putting sections of railway out of action, but these were only temporary gains as within a few months the Japanese had recaptured all they had lost and rebuilt their forts more strongly. Communist officers a few years later were admitting that the offensive had been a mistake. For momentary advantage they had suffered extremely heavy casualties and used most of their reserves of ammunition. One Japanese officer I talked with in 1961 had been on the planning staff of the North China Army Headquarters and described the Hundred Regiment Campaign as the one major mistake of the Chinese Communists. The recent official Chinese Communist line explains it by megalomania on the part of P'eng Te-huai, which leaves unexplained why other leaders approved it at the time unless the motives were only political and intended to turn Chinese public opinion against a possible compromise between the National Government and the rival Japanese sponsored regime set up by Wang Ching-wei in March 1940. Kuomintang propaganda was started to make accusations that the Communists were not fighting the Japanese and the offensive would refute these charges. War time relations between the Communists and the Kuomintang are highly complicated and controversial. The united front worked fairly effectively in 1938 when Nationalist troops under General Lu Chung-lin were going through the Communist base area to take over South Hopei, where the countryside had been held by the Communists in the spring.

Communist officers spoke with some respect of Lu Chung-lin, calling him a genuine patriot who really wished to fight the Japanese but whose old fashioned ideas on organisation made him unable to resist the serious Japanese offensive against him in 1939. They had no such respect for one of his subordinates, Chang Yin-wu, whom they denounced as the originator of the slogan, "Crooked line save country," which meant co-operating with the Japanese to oppose the Communists.

Some accounts date the breakdown of the united front from the New Fourth Army incident of January 1941. In fact this was merely the first fighting between Kuomintang and Communist forces which both sides decided to make public. Quite serious clashes had begun in 1939 and once the Japanese stepped up pressure in North China only a high degree of mutual trust could have prevented trouble between Kuomintang and Communist forces in the same general area, Japanese offensives pressured the local Chinese forces to move and since their styles of military organisation and civilian government were so different their areas were not interchangeable. In fact political developments reduced local mutual confidence. The defection of Wang Ching-wei, a leading figure in the Kuomintang, made the Communists suspect that the National Government might come to terms with the Japanese while uncritical Communist support of the Nazi-Soviet Pact increased Kuomintang suspicions that the Communists were really controlled by the Soviet Union.

By the end of 1943 Kuomintang forces had largely disappeared north of the Yellow River — which after 1938 ran on a new course south of Shantung. The standard pattern of military and civil organisation which the National Government tried to enforce was not suited to resist the heavy and continuous Japanese pressure. Between 1941 and 1943 many Kuomintang units in North China surrendered to the Japanese and were then incorporated in Wang

Attack on Japanese fort.

Ching-wei's pro-Japanese organisation. A number of Kuomintang units did survive in Shantung until they were eliminated by the Communists in 1945 but their organisation was much closer to the Communist model since certain practical features of organisation are essential if a resistance movement is to survive against an enemy with superior equipment and fire power.

From the end of 1940 to the end of 1943 the Japanese were gaining in North China. The number of Communist troops fell by about a quarter and the loss of their more fertile territories to the fort and blockade line system forced the Communist base areas to make drastic economies and to increase their rates of taxation.

The weakness of the fort and blockade line strategy was in the huge demands it made on manpower. In 1943 the Japanese had roughly thirty thousand forts in China each probably needing about twenty men. There also had to be widely distributed reserves ready to reinforce any fort under attack, and still more troops were needed for the destructive campaigns against the base areas. Much of the fort system was garrisoned by Chinese troops in Japanese service, making it far less effective. The Communists were able to arrange "live and let live" agreements with many puppet units. General Huang Yung-sheng of Chin-Ch'a-Chi 3rd. sub-district told me that permission from his headquarters was needed for an attack on a puppet garrison.

The crossing from Central Hopei to the base area west of the railway involved a night march of some thirty miles through a closely spaced fort and blockade line system. People who had made the crossing often reported no opposition, and once when a party reported some shooting, a farmer came next morning with a message from the puppet troops saying that although they had to fire because there were Japanese with them, they hoped that no one had been hurt.

One student in my radio engineering course had a similar story. He had been with a unit in Central Hopei whose machine gun had broken down, and they sent a farmer with a message to a local puppet garrison asking for the loan of a machine gun while theirs was repaired. After a little argument the puppet troops agreed to lend a gun if its return was guaranteed before the next possible Japanese inspection in ten days' time.

If the Japanese had been able to continue their fort and blockade line strategy for several more years and if they had been able to garrison all their forts with reliable troops they could have perhaps reduced the Communists in North China to an underground organisation and a few scattered guerilla bands in the mountains. They had been able to eliminate overt resistance in Manchuria though their strategy there was to concentrate the population in fortified villages with Japanese garrisons. In fact, after 1943 when they had to withdraw troops from North China to meet the demands of the war in the Pacific, the whole system began to collapse. In July 1943 the Communists held only two *hsien* cities in North China. Fup'ing in Chin-Ch'a-Chi and P'inghsun in the mountains of Southeast Shansi. By July 1944 they held over forty and, by 1945, the Japanese were back to their positions of early 1938, holding only the railways.

Talking with former Japanese officers I have found them rather proud of their efforts against the Communist forces and inclined to argue that they had been much more effective than the Americans in Vietnam. However in judging the Communist war effort against the Japanese one should allow for the fact that they got no outside supplies at all from 1940 and very little even before this. For weapons and ammunition they had to rely on what they could capture from the Japanese or what they could produce in primitive local arsenals. Sulphuric acid was manufactured in Chin-Ch'a-Chi by the old lead chamber process using the large earthenware vessels in which farmers stored grain as reaction chambers. The Japanese took increasing precautions to avoid the loss of ammunition so that, by the 1940's, the only weapons in reasonably good supply were hand grenades and land mines. One sub-district commander told me that only soldiers with a special marksman's qualification were allowed to open fire at more than one hundred yards. Considering this shortage the Communist performance was remarkable.

Compared with Communist insurgencies in Southeast Asia, neither the terrain nor the climate favoured guerilla fighting. The mountain areas are certainly wild and had no roads, but except in parts of Northwest Shansi, the mountains are bare. There is nothing like the thick jungle cover of guerilla base areas in Vietnam or Malaya, while Central Hopei is a flat plain which could easily be traversed by the enemy's motorized equipment except during the rainy season.

In Southeast Asia, guerilla forces can survive in the open if necessary and need only simple shelter against rain for comparative comfort. In the North China winter both shelter and warmth were essential for survival. On the plains, night temperatures would be below freezing from December through February, and in the mountains the winter was longer and temperatures could reach fourteen degrees below zero at Yenan. The Japanese admitted that the climate had been an important help in their supression of any open insurgency in Manchuria. Once they had forced the population to concentrate in fortified villages and destroyed all other housing, guerilla forces could not survive.

In compensation the Chinese Communist forces had the genuine and active support of the local population. Unlike the Communists in Vietnam and Malaya they had no need to use terrorism to secure co-operation from the people. How they won this support is considered in more detail later.

Yenching campus.

My study at Yenching.

Yenching University, 1937.

My connection with China began in 1937. I had finished a job as Assistant Director of the Second Industrial Survey of South Wales and was looking for another. Meanwhile, people at Yenching near Peking which, like most Chinese universities, had been organized on the American system with credits and grades, were thinking of an experiment along the lines of the Oxford Tutorial system, with most of the money to come from the Universities China Committee, a body that handled the British Boxer indemnity money. Wu Wen-tsao, the Professor of Sociology, came to England looking for two people to help start the experiment. An obvious choice was George Taylor who had already taught in China; for the second he made enquiries from W. A. L. Adams, Warden of All Souls, a friend of my father who knew that I was looking for a job and suggested that I might be both suitable and interested. I knew little about China but I was very interested and accepted. Although the fighting had started in China and the future existence of Yenching seemed doubtful I arranged to travel via the United States where I could make some study of experiments there in introducing tutorial systems and finally left for China in December 1937, sailing from Vancouver to Yokohama and travelling to Peking, then called Peip'ing, through Korea and Manchuria. A fellow passenger with whom I became friends was Dr. Norman Bethune who has become a national hero in Canada. We never expected to meet again because I was going to the Japanese occupied area and he to the unoccupied.

These were taken in the Forbidden City (the old imperial palace) in the winter of 1938-9. The long Chinese gowns as men's wear have disappeared but the buildings remain unchanged.

The tutorial experiment was interesting and the students, selected by a competitive examination, seemed to enjoy the system. We reckoned that, when we had worked up to our full complement of students, our staffing ratio would only be slightly above the rest of the university. Of course classes in the American system were much larger than our small tutorial groups, but grades and credits required far more time spent on administrative work. What made the tutorial system more expensive was the necessity for more highly trained teachers. A junior instructor could get up the material required to teach an American style course but a tutor had to be able to deal with students' questions on anything related to the general subject.

Apart from all this Yenching from 1937 to 1941 was an intriguing place and the only free university in China. It had been started in 1926 from the union of several small protestant missionary colleges in Peking and the new site was five or six miles outside the city walls on the way to the Summer Palace. The buildings were of foreign construction but had Chinese exteriors with upward curling roofs and the interiors, though westernized and with every modern convenience, had beautiful Chinese furniture. The West Gate of the campus was painted brilliant red and immediately through this was a hump-backed bridge over a stream full of gold fish which flowed from the Wu Ming lake into lotus ponds. There were marble pillars carved with dragons from the old Imperial Summer Palace. The water tower, a landmark, was built in pagoda style and, in the centre of the campus, at the highest point, was the president's house, behind which was the Yenching lake. The garden, part of which had been a Manchu prince's, had weeping willows, forsythia and then apricot, plum and peach blossom; it was covered in flowers until winter. A missionary university, registered in the State of New York, Yenching enjoyed extra-territorial status which the Japanese and the new Reformed Government of China respected. As a matter of principle we took no notice of any educational regulations issued by the Japanese sponsored Reformed Government. In theory we owed allegiance to the Ministry of Education in the National Government but they were pleased to have any university in the occupied areas acknowledging their authority and had no means of actual control. In 1939 Ch'en Li-fu, the Minister of Education, issued a set of regulations designed to prevent political activity by students in unoccupied China, keeping them in the class room for over thirty hours a week. When these reached Yenching a faculty meeting was called. Everyone said that the new regulations were impossible, so we picked out a few points which could be observed without much trouble to save face for Ch'en Li-fu and ignored the rest.

The University President, Dr. J. Leighton Stuart, was particularly skilful in dealing with the Japanese. He was accommodating on unimportant matters of detail. To prevent Japanese soldiers straying on to the campus the university put up notices in Japanese saying that it was American property, but when the Japanese objected, the notices were changed to English, Chinese and Japanese. On important issues he would say that he could not prevent the Japanese from closing down the university but would not compromise on principle. The Japanese asked the foreign owned universities to admit Japanese students. When Fu Jen, the Catholic University, yielded on this the students turned out to be Japanese army agents and a general nuisance. Dr. Stuart's reaction was to make sure that he could prove that the professors who marked the entrance examination had no means of knowing whose papers they were marking. When no Japanese students were admitted and the Japanese protested he was able to show that more than fifty Chinese students who had not been admitted had done better than the best Japanese candidate. Since the entrance examination required proficiency in both Chinese and English it would have been hard to find Japanese candidates who could have won admission on their merits. On a larger scale the French successfully used the same strategies to defend their interests in China. The French government had far less real power behind it in China than the Americans, less even than the British, but they were not afraid to use this power. The Japanese knew that, if they interfered with French interests, the French would retaliate, forcing the Japanese to choose between backing down or escalating the disagreement to a definite act of war against France. Until the French collapse in 1940 they always backed down.

Central Hopei, Easter 1938.

The AP correspondent in Peking, Haldore Hanson, visiting Central Hopei in early 1938 reported that an interesting organisation was developing there and three young foreign teachers, including myself, decided to take a look during the Easter vacation. I had recently bought a good camera, a Zeiss Ikon 3.5, taking 16 on 120 film, which was the one I used throughout my years in China. It was a particular bargain bought with the North China Federal Reserve Bank dollar set up by the Japanese who were pretending it was worth a yen when in fact it was worth about one third. Serge Vargasoff, a White Russian, developed and printed my film in Peking but once we had joined the Communist guerillas after 1942, my film had to be developed by army technicians in the field — which meant primitive makeshift darkrooms with no running water.

At that time there was no problem in crossing from Japanese to Chinese territory so we took our bicycles on the train to Pao-ting, about one hundred and fifty miles south of Peking, and bicycled out into the countryside. After perhaps two miles we passed the last Japanese sentries and, about a mile further on, came to the first Chinese sentries. Travel was easy at this time of year. In North China from October to June the sky is usually cloudless, the occasional winter snowfalls have evaporated without melting and spring rains, though important for agriculture, are seldom heavy

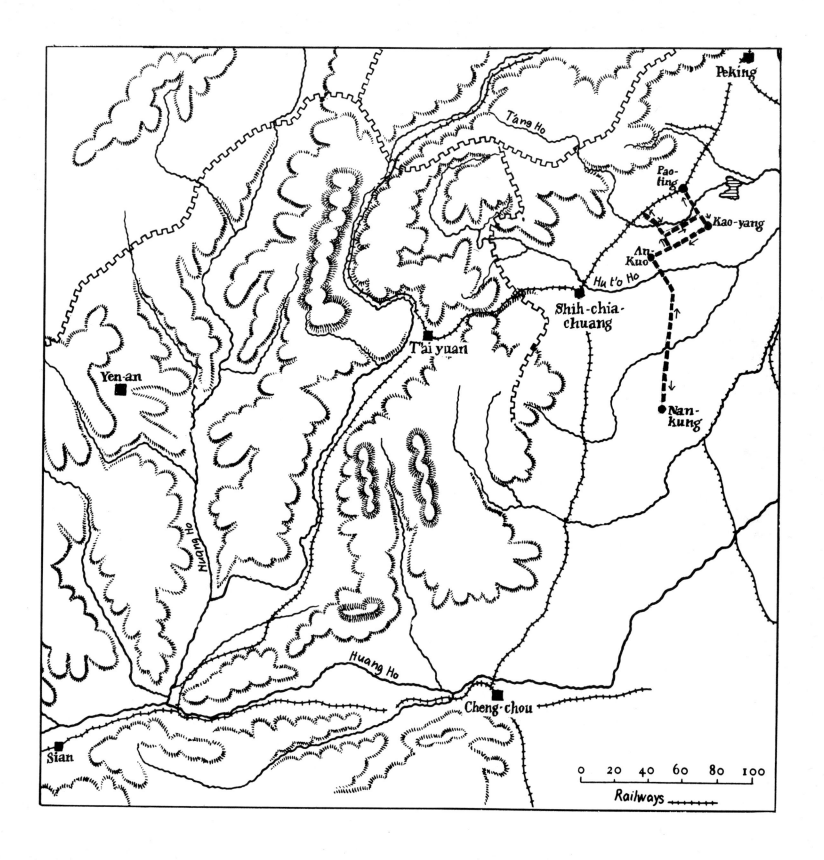

Soldiers playing volleyball outside *hsien* in Central Hopei.

or long lasting. For parts of our journey we were taken by lorry and although bicycling was sometimes difficult because of deep dust one could usually find a firm path along the edge of the road.

Foreign visitors were considered good publicity and we were given VIP treatment and taken on a tour of the area. Everywhere anti-Japanese meetings were being held and newly recruited troops being drilled. At that time Lü Cheng-ts'ao's troops did not call themselves Eighth Route Army, because of the public's lingering suspicion of Communism, but had khaki uniforms with armbands inscribed: "Central Hopei People's Self Defence Army". I remember one strange breakfast when the local general had decided that foreign visitors should have foreign food. The actual food was correct, fried eggs and toasted steamed bread, but they also served beer and brandy — a half empty glass of beer would be filled up with brandy and *vice versa*.

We were invited to join in a raid on the Peking-Hankow railway and were able to see that the army, at this time, was not very competent. The unit we accompanied marched by day to a village five or ten miles from the railway and after dark set off on what should have been an easy night march, going due east across a flat plain. However a brief dust storm came up and the officers lost their way — they did not know how to find north from the stars and we wandered round for most of the night only reaching the railway at first light to damage two or three rails before making a hasty retreat.

Eighth Route Army troops, Wu-t'ai area.

Central Hopei.

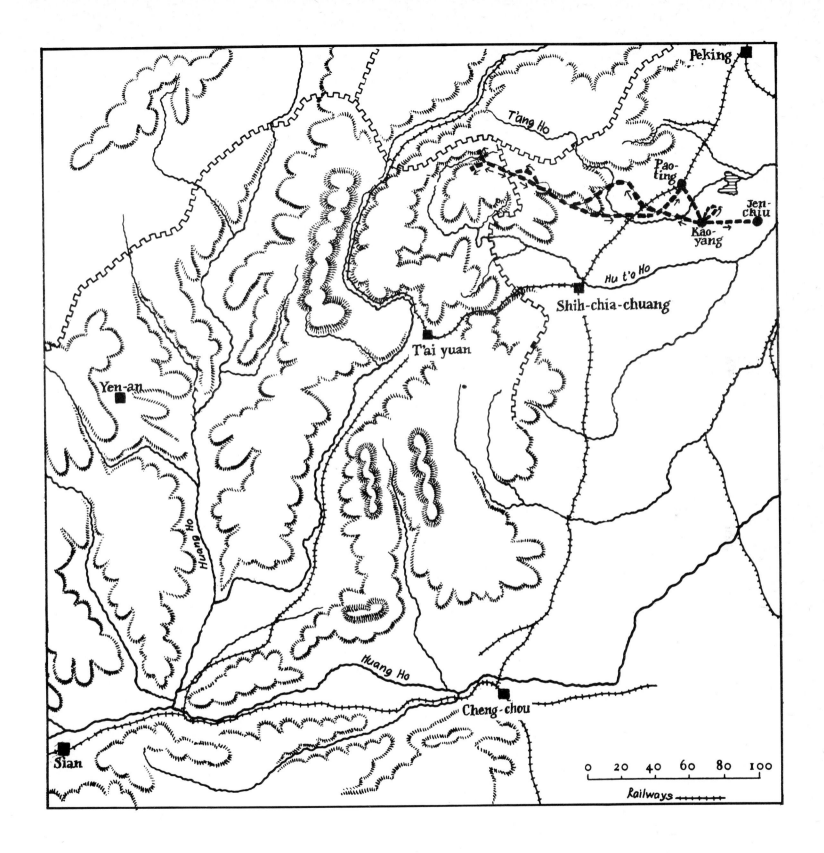

Peking

T'ang Ho

Pao-ting

Jen-chiu

Kao-yang

Hu t'o Ho

Shih-chia-chuang

T'ai yuan

Yen-an

Huang Ho

Huang Ho

Cheng-chou

Sian

0   20   40   60   80   100

Railways +++++++

Chin-Ch'a-Chi, Summer 1938.

In the summer vacation of 1938 I made a more extended trip with George Taylor, my colleague in the tutorial scheme. Again starting in Central Hopei, we were welcomed by a brass band as we entered Lü Cheng-ts'ao's headquarters at Jen-ch'iu and were then escorted across the Peking-Hankow railway to the main Chin-Ch'a-Chi headquarters of General Nieh Jung-chen and the civilian government under Sung Shao-wen which were in Shansi in the Wu-t'ai mountains. This was the rainy season, we had to cross flooded areas by boat in Central Hopei, and in the mountains forded a succession of flooded rivers where the water might be up to one's waist with a strong current. I learnt a great deal more from this trip because by this time, I could understand Chinese and George Taylor spoke it well.

Spring 1938. Old guns, presumably abandoned, in Central Hopei during one of the early warlord civil wars.

Spring 1938. Slogans on wall of local Headquarters. Left triangle "Struggle to protect our homeland", left vertical "America is a loveable, peaceful country", right vertical "Japan is the enemy of mankind", right triangle "Strengthen the power of the world peace front".

Flooded areas in Central Hopei. Summer 1938.

Flooded areas in Central Hopei. Summer 1938.

Making uniforms.

Locally made hand grenades and mortar shells.

Local arsenal, Central Hopei.

Rifle made in this arsenal.

Parade to welcome Michael Lindsay and George Taylor at General Lü Cheng-ts'ao's Headquarters at Jen-ch'iu.

Mass meeting at Jen-Ch'iu.

Stop for tea on our journey, Central Hopei.

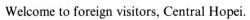

Welcome to foreign visitors, Central Hopei.

Staff of sub-district Headquarters, Central Hopei.

Welcome to foreign visitors, Central Hopei.

Writing out orders, Central Hopei.

Small boys as army messengers, Central Hopei.

Our escort for crossing Peking-Hankow railway from Central Hopei to Wu-t'ai.

Rest stop at village school, Central Hopei.

Village school, Central Hopei. Characters on blackboard, left to right, "you", "I", "farmer", "man", "study", "do", "work".

Members of our escort, Central Hopei.

On the way towards the hills west of the Peking-Hankow railway.

George Taylor reviews parade at T'ang-hsien.

Fording Sha River.

Ford on T'ang River.

Youth organisation welcomes foreign visitors.

Stop for tea and a wash.

Small boys on sentry duty.

Japanese prisoners.

Damage from Japanese attack.

Typical village temple.

The Sha River at Fu-p'ing.

On the way to Lung-ch'uan-kuan (dragon spring pass) between Hopei and Shansi.

Old fortifications at Lung-ch'uan-kuan.

The town of Lung-ch'uan-kuan.

Bridge in Wu-t'ai area.

Anti-Japanese drama at Wu-t'ai.

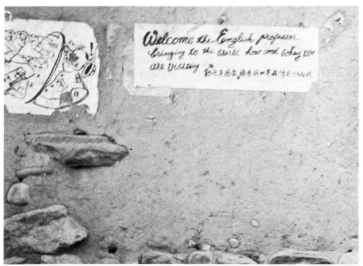

Welcoming poster.

Meal time of organisation at Chin-Ch'a-Chi Headquarters at Wu-t'ai.

Troops on march in Wu-t'ai area.

Troops on march in West Hopei village.

General Nieh Jung-chen addressing mass meeting of troops at Wu-t'ai.

Michael Lindsay with Sung Shao-wen (Chairman of Chin-Ch'a-Chi government) and two members of his staff.

National Government troops of General Lu Chung-lin at Wu-t'ai on their way to take over South Hopei.

Eighth Route Army troops at Wu-t'ai.

Bank of Chin-Ch'a-Chi.Wut'ai.

Printing new Chin Ch'a Chi currency. This kept out the National Government notes which the Japanese had got in exchange for their new Federal Reserve Bank notes.

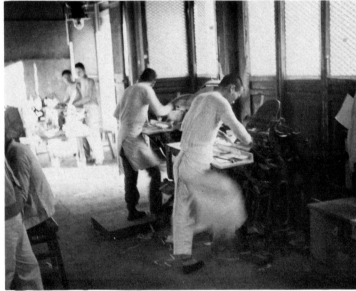

Curious crowd looking at foreigner.

Village school, West Hopei.

Curious crowd looking at foreigners. Some small children were frightened by the camera.

Dr. Bethune's interpreter, General Nieh Jung-chen, Dr. Bethune.

Dr. Norman Bethune.

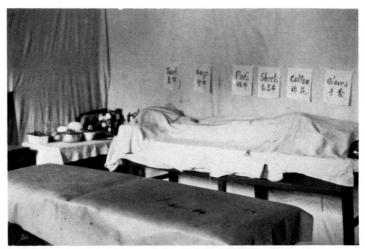

Operating theatre at Dr. Bethune's hospital.

Michael Lindsay on journey with Dr. Bethune from General Nieh's Headquarters to Dr. Bethune's hospital.

Treating patient at Dr. Bethune's hospital.

The village where Dr. Bethune had his hospital.

Stretcher party carrying wounded soldier to Dr. Bethune's hospital.

Mountain scenery, Wu-t'ai area

My escort for unsuccessful attempt to cross Peking-Hankow railway.

After crossing Peking-Hankow railway. The bag contains my Western clothes and my two escort's uniforms. They carried Mauser pistols under their shirts.

Station on railway from Pei-tai-ho to Peking damaged by July 1938 rising in East Hopei.

I was impressed by the Chinese Communists and compared them very favourably with the Communists I had known in England who were extremely doctrinaire, losing their tempers if one tried to argue with them. Also when I had been working in South Wales, I had found the local Communists opposed any attempts to help the unemployed miners on the grounds that this would make them less revolutionary. Here the Communists seemed reasonable people and what they were doing was obviously helping the ordinary peasants.

Wu-t'ai.

At Wu-t'ai I again met Dr. Norman Bethune whose base hospital was in the area. He cured us both of dysentery by administering calomel followed by opium. (This was the treatment prescribed in Manson's *Tropical Medicine* before the development of anti-biotics.) George Taylor wished to get back to his family but I stayed on and spent a week with Dr. Bethune. His hospital was a farm courtyard with the wounded on *k'angs* in the rooms round it — a *k'ang* is a raised platform for sleeping and sitting which is heated from underneath by a flue. Dr. Bethune was an enthusiastic and rather unsophisticated Communist. He told me that he had become one because of a visit to the Soviet Union during which he had been impressed by their treatment of TB. I was able to observe two of Dr. Bethune's characteristics — his devotion to the care of his patients and refusal to tolerate anything that caused them unnecessary suffering, and his inability to learn languages. Some wounded had come to the hospital and the man in charge did not notify Bethune until several hours later so he had to make his first inspection by the feeble light of a vegetable oil lamp. He was furious and later called in the man responsible, cursed him for five or ten minutes and ended by saying that, had he done that in Canada he would have been dismissed immediately and never got another job in medical work. The interpreters translated this long tirade by saying, "Dr. Bethune is not too satisfied with your behaviour." Even in 1939 when he had lived for more than a year in an environment where only his interpreter spoke English he could still only manage a few very simple phrases such as *k'ai fan* (serve food).

In 1938 he deplored the situation in which all his patients had to travel by stretcher for a week or more before they reached him, so that the wounds had become infected. When I saw him again in 1939 he was just back from Central Hopei where he had been working with operating equipment that could be carried by two pack mules. This enabled him to operate and apply casts or dressings within a few miles of the actual fighting — on certain occasions his team had moved out of one end of the village as the Japanese entered at the other.

The most exciting part of the trip was the return to Central Hopei across the Peking — Hankow railway. On the way to Wu-t'ai, George Taylor and I with our escort had made an uneventful night crossing on horseback but I only managed the return crossing on the fourth attempt. I set off on the first night with an escort of about a dozen men, but we had to turn back when we discovered that another party had raided the railway and cut the telegraph wires so a Japanese armoured train was patrolling the line. This failure was apparently considered a loss of face because the next night I was given an additional escort of over a hundred men. They were to go ahead and scout along the railway. It was a bright moonlit night and my immediate party had white horses. We approached the railway in the cover of a sunken road but the last quarter mile or so was across a flat field with very low crops. Luckily the man in charge of me was an old Red Army veteran who distrusted the scouting ability of the new recruits. He went about a hundred yards ahead and, when he looked over a low embankment on to the railway, found a party of Japanese on the other side. We had to crawl back to cover with bullets whistling overhead. The Japanese were also inexperienced; the only person hurt was a soldier who was trying to mount his horse as a bullet hit the stirrup and twisted his ankle.

The next morning I was surprised when I woke to find that breakfast was ready. Usually people only prepared a meal when you were waiting for it, but my escort explained that a Japanese armoured train was moving along the railway shelling the villages and any moment was due to start on the one we were in. Our attempt to cross that night was also a failure since a heavy thunderstorm had flooded a small stream we had to cross. When I suggested that we could cross in daytime because the Japanese were not patrolling the line strictly, this was finally agreed on. I was dressed in borrowed Chinese farmer's clothing; two soldiers escorting me also changed into plain clothes with Mauser pistols under their shirts and carried a sack with their uniforms and my Western clothes. We had no more trouble, walked through a village where a Japanese flag flew over a sentry and, about two miles east of the railway, were safely back in Chinese held territory.

Pei Chu Ma Ho in flood which held us up for nine days and kept General Hsiao K'e on the other side.

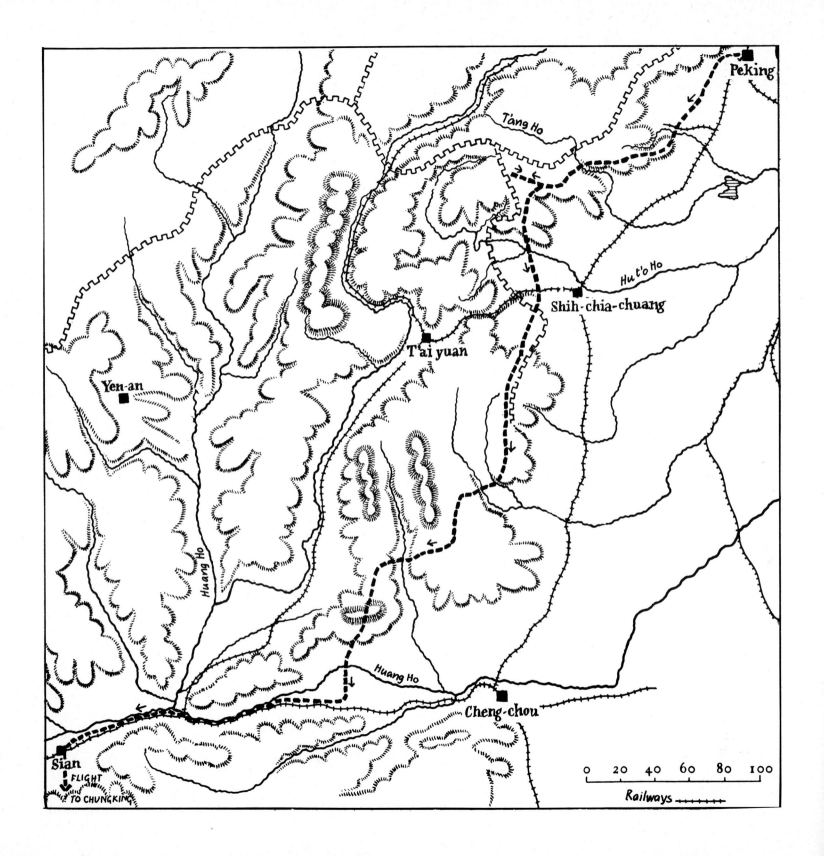

Peking

T'ang Ho

Hu t'o Ho

Shih-chia-chuang

T'ai yuan

Yen-an

Huang Ho

Huang Ho

Cheng-chou

Sian

FLIGHT

TO CHUNGKING

0   20   40   60   80   100

Railways +++++++

Yenching University, 1938.

On my return I became more deeply involved in working for the anti-Japanese underground in Peking. I had given some help before because it was clear that any thinking person had a duty to oppose the Japanese army and a foreigner could do a lot by reason of his extra-territorial rights. Foreigners, for example, were not searched at the gates of Peking. I often bought medical supplies and went on to buying wireless parts as requested by my contacts, adding certain items on my own initiative; in a book store in Tung An Shih Chang I found a large textbook on the manufacture of explosives.

To avoid possible trouble to the shops where I made my purchases it was desirable to remove the original labels and it seemed best to relabel medical supplies in Chinese. For help in this I turned to a student in one of my tutorial classes whom I judged to be trustworthy. In 1941 she became my wife.

Chin-Ch'a-Chi, Summer 1939.

In the summer of 1939 I made another, longer trip through the Communist areas, this time in a party of four. My companions were Ralph Lapwood, mathematics professor at Yenching who had decided to work for the Chinese Industrial Co-operatives in unoccupied China, Chao Ming, a former Yenching student who had been working for the underground in Peking but was moving to Chin-Ch'a-Chi, and Hsiao Ts'ai-t'ien, a workman from the Yenching power station who went with Lapwood but later returned to Peking. Hsiao was an extremely skilful mechanic. When my camera had fallen into a flooded river he took the shutter mechanism to pieces, cleaned and put it together with no tools but a pocket knife. He had very little regular education and on one occasion, wanting to divide a number by ten wrote it out as a long division sum. When he went back to Peking, Hsiao Ts'ai-t'ien worked for the anti-Japanese underground and was arrested and tortured by the Kempetai. A week or so after his arrest someone came to me and said that they had contacted the Kempetai commandant at Hsi-yuan who had agreed to release Hsiao in return for enough money to buy himself a new motorcycle. I contributed to the fund and shortly afterwards he was released.

Youth organisation, P'inghsi.

This time we started through the Western Hills and tried to look like a picnic party celebrating the Moon Festival as we went through the Japanese post at Wen-ch'uan. The rainy season of 1939 produced serious floods and we were held up by the high rivers. On reaching General Hsiao K'e's Headquarters in P'inghsi we found that the general was stuck on the other side of the Pei Chu Ma Ho but after a week a boat was constructed from a set of wooden boxes tied together with rope, and he was able to return.

The next day, or the day after, we made the crossing in the other direction. The current was very swift and swung from one bank to the other so the people paddling the boat had to get out of the current at the right point. We crossed safely but the next party

Youth organisation sentries.

Village in mountains.

Village militia.

wanting to go in the other direction missed their chance of reaching land and were swept out of sight. When I next crossed this river in January 1942 one could step over it.

Though little over a hundred miles from Peking as the plane flies, the country there was extremely primitive. The women arranged their hair in Ming dynasty style and the soldiers told us that, when they arrived in 1938, several villages had not heard of the Republic and were using dates from the last emperor. (The traditional Chinese system, which the Japanese still use, gives the emperor's name and the date of his reign.)

After another week's travel we arrived at General Nieh Jungchen's Headquarters where we met Dr. Bethune. He badly needed a holiday and a change to foreign food and English speaking company and I suggested that he could follow the route we had used and offered to put him up in safety at Yenching until he could arrange travel to Shanghai or Hongkong. Unfortunately he never did this, and a few months later he died of blood poisoning. He cut his finger while operating and the wound became infected. His chief assistant told us later that he had urged Bethune to have his finger amputated but Bethune refused because it would have crippled him as a surgeon.

Our original plan had been to visit Yenan but the military situation made this nearly impossible. We had to wait for about two weeks in a small village near the Hopei-Shansi border and then went on to 4th. sub-district Headquarters to join a party of troops crossing the Shih-chia-chuang-T'aiyuan railway to Southeast Shansi. While there we heard the news of the outbreak of war in Europe.

Southeast Shansi.

The crossing of this railway was quite uneventful and took us into a very different country from Chin-Ch'a-Chi. We climbed through wild mountains with deep gorges on to the loess plateau and after travelling about a week reached the main Eighth Route Army Headquarters and met General Chu Te.

My clearest recollection of this meeting is the charm with which Chu Te put Hsiao Ts'ai-t'ien at ease. After they had talked a little Hsiao explained that he had felt somewhat embarassed at other headquarters in the presence of highly educated people. With Chu Te he felt completely at ease and gave him a long lecture on the way the Eighth Route Army ill treated its machinery.

On the way to crossing of Shih-chia-chuang – T'aiyuan railway.

Southeast Shansi landscape. At the top of the gorge one came out on to loess plateau.

A few more days' journey took us into territory controlled by National Government troops. Although clashes had started in some areas between Kuomintang and Communists the united front still seemed to be working here. We crossed the Yellow River at a busy ferry point and another day's journey brought us to the Lunghai railway. In the last ten days we had marched roughly two hundred and fifty miles and Lapwood kept a diary of our movements, reckoning that we had walked altogether about a thousand miles.

We travelled by train to Sian though we had to walk across a gap of some ten miles near T'ung-kuan where the line was under artillery fire from the Japanese on the north bank. After a few days at Sian I managed to get a flight to Chungking, another to Hongkong and a boat via Shanghai which got me to Tientsin and so back to Yenching. The journey had taken far longer than expected and I had missed more than a month of the autumn term. Many people thought that I must have been killed as my father had telegraphed President Leighton Stuart to enquire about me, having never received the telegram I had sent from Sian.

Chungking, 1940.

Because of the war, the British funds for the tutorial experiment were going to end with the academic year 1939-40 and I therefore accepted an offer from the British Ambassador to become British Press Attaché at Chungking.

The Ambassador, Sir Archibald Clarke-Kerr, was one of the more impressive people in the British service. Unlike many other diplomatists he was really interested in complete information. When he visited Peking he had an introduction to Dr. Leighton Stuart with whom he became good friends and did not confine his contacts to regular diplomatic circles but arranged meetings with representatives of the Japanese sponsored government and of both the Kuomintang and the Communist underground organisations.

I spent a few weeks in Shanghai and Hongkong and then flew to Chungking. During this period I had no contacts with Chou En-lai's liaison office there because relations between the British and the Chinese Communists had seriously deteriorated. This was the period of the Nazi-Soviet pact and the *Hsin Hua Jih Pao,* the Communist paper in Chungking, published frequent and vituperative attacks on the allies while only occasionally making very mild criticisms of Hitler. I was quite often instructed to make official protests to the Chinese government about these articles.

Chungking in the summer of 1940 still retained some of the patriotic enthusiasm of the early years of the war. From most accounts, the atmosphere became far more depressing in later years. Working conditions were difficult, partly because of the climate, it was often ninety-five degrees at midnight with intense humidity, and partly because of air raids. To begin with the Japanese used only high explosive and did limited damage, though the British Embassy building took a direct hit. Later they shifted to incendiaries and almost the whole of downtown Chungking became ruins. The Japanese still did not want to annoy the Americans and declared a safety zone on the south bank round the American Embassy which they observed except for a few mistakes around the edges, and this made it possible to sit in almost complete safety watching a full scale air raid only half a mile away. One American honeymoon couple actually visited Chungking for the spectacle.

The Chinese were almost helpless against these raids though an excellent system of shelters had been dug into the rock after one raid in 1939 caused heavy casualties. There were a handful of anti-aircraft guns and a few obsolete fighters, slower on the level than the Japanese bombers but a most efficient warning system. The first warning came more than an hour before the raid when bombers left their base, the second to show they were headed for Chungking gave about fifteen minutes notice when everyone was supposed to go into the shelters. At the British Embassy we had a shelter in the garden so everyone moved out to near the entrance and read or played bridge until someone detailed as observer saw the planes approaching.

British Embassy building after bombing.

Chungking 1940.

Fires at night, Chungking.

Firefighting, Chungking.

long delays and colossal expense by obtaining Japanese permission to ship it to Shanghai, shipping it from Shanghai to Rangoon and finally moving it to Chungking by the Burma road. My favourite story about British bureaucracy concerns a specially made wireless receiver which was sent to all Press Attachés. This looked very impressive with a grey-painted steel panel with a milliameter — but the milliameter showed nothing except even harmonic distortion in the output stage. There was a converter for receiving telegraphed news broadcasts from Rugby on about 20 kHz but the short wave part of the set had a circuit of the cheapest type of all-wave receiver and, even by this standard, was badly designed. It drifted through 3 or 4 channels on the 10 MHz band as it warmed up and when London was coming through at full strength on a good ordinary broadcast receiver the Ambassador had bought in Hongkong, the special set designed by the Foreign Office gave a barely intelligible signal which often faded out completely.

I wrote a scathing report on this with some suggestions about the kind of design needed and sent it to my boss in Hongkong, who passed it on. When he later visited London he asked the official responsible if he had seen my report. The official apparently replied that my criticisms were quite unjustified, and proceeded to demonstrate that it could receive London Regional in London. My boss asked for a demonstration that it could receive some short wave station from Asia but prolonged attempts to do this failed completely. Then came the truly egregious remark, "Would you believe it? We have sent out more than ninety of these sets and, almost everyone has complained about them."

Yenching University, September 1940.

Dr. Leighton Stuart wished the tutorial experiment to continue. He managed to raise extra money and asked the Ambassador to allow me to return to Yenching. George Taylor had left in 1939 to become the head of the Sino-Soviet Institute at the University of Washington in Seattle so I was the only professor in the scheme with actual experience of tutorial teaching when I returned to Yenching in September 1940.

It was one of the curious things about the war in China that communication between the two sides was never fully shut off. Up to December 1941 there was regular travel via Hongkong. Even later, travel between Peking and Chungking was not particularly difficult for Chinese citizens. One took the train to Chengchow, walked across some twenty miles of no-man's land through the country devastated by the Yellow River floods of 1938 and was then in National Government territory. In 1942 many of the Chinese faculty moved to restart Yenching on the campus of the West China University at Chengtu and as late as 1943 one could post a letter in Peking and get a reply from Chungking within about six weeks. The Chinese Post Office prided itself on delivering letters anywhere in China and treated the Sino-Japanese war as it had previously treated civil wars.

I had the impression that British official organisation was less efficient than that of the Chinese Communists. Some officials were extremely competent but others were quite unsuited for the conditions in China. They were often intelligent and hard working but completely inhibited by convention. When the Japanese army interfered with British interests they complained to officials of the Japanese consular service, although everyone knew that the Japanese Foreign Office was completely powerless to control the army. When a message came to Chungking from Sir Archibald Clarke-Kerr to tell Chiang Kai-shek that Dr. Leighton Stuart had had a serious riding accident and was not yet out of danger, this produced a reply that the message should go through the American authorities since Leighton Stuart was an American citizen. In 1949 I met the son of M. Egal who had headed the Free French movement in Shanghai. He told me that, when the Ambassador was in Chungking, the British authorities in Shanghai had refused to have any dealings with his father on the grounds that he represented a rebel government. They also refused to take action when his father was kidnapped by the pro-Vichy authorities of the French Concession in Shanghai, and sent to Haiphong to be tried for treason. However, as soon as he heard of this, the Ambassador acted to save M. Egal.

Many officials in London seemed even more hopelessly bureaucratic. When we needed more furniture the Office of Works suggested we take unused furniture from the British Embassy building in Nanking. It was theoretically possible to get this with

Our wedding at Yenching, Hsiao Li's parents at back. Front row; my best man, Rudolf Loewenthal, Michael Lindsay, Hsiao Li, bridesmaid, Han Ch'iu-feng.

Our wedding party.

Lindsay's wedding.

In May 1941 I became engaged to Li Hsiao-li, the student who had been helping me with my underground work and we were married on 25th, June 1941.

My father-in-law was a retired Colonel from the Shansi Provincial Army. The family fortunes had been founded by an ancestor who had been a general under the Mánchus and the Lis had become the leading family of Li-shih, a small town in Western Shansi. My father-in-law had broken with the family to go to the officers training school at Pao-ting, established by Yuan Shih-k'ai to modernize the Chinese army. He was too honest to be really successful in a warlord army. My wife said that he was always beloved and respected by his subordinates but never sufficiently respectful to his superiors, and strongly disapproved of the Chinese custom of giving presents. At one time he had been chief of staff to General Fu Tso-i but he had retired in the early 1930's. When war started with Japan, he had been afraid that, if he remained at home, he would be pressed to serve in the Japanese sponsored administration and had moved, first to Tientsin where my future brother-in-law was with the Bank of China and later to a village adjoining Yenching to be near his daughter.

Hsiao Li had been one of the representatives of her class at junior middle school in T'aiyuan during the anti-Japanese demonstrations of the mid-1930's and the Minister of Education, who was a family friend, warned that she would be arrested if she remained in Shansi. She finished middle school in Peking and was planning to go to Ginling University in Nanking. The war with Japan made this impossible but Yenching held an extra examination for admission in which she was successful.

Wang Yu and his wife. Head of enemy area intelligence Chin-Ch'a-Chi, January 1942, P'inghsi. I took him into Peking on my motorcycle in 1941.

The pace of work for the anti-Japanese organisation increased during 1941. On several occasions I borrowed Dr. Stuart's car to take loads of supplies into the countryside, and we also made preparations for the moment when we ourselves might have to escape into the mountains, buying a couple of rucksacks and rubber mattresses, some winter clothes and medicines which we kept hidden in Peking, and taking a wooden box Hsiao-Li had packed with ten pounds of sugar, a five pound tin of Klim, cocoa, tins of jams and several pairs of thick socks.

Once I was asked to help in getting someone into Peking. My contacts explained that, once he was in the city, they had arrangements with a Japanese officer who would sell him a resident's pass. The problem was getting him through the gate. I said that the Japanese had never stopped my motorcycle and if he sat on the back dressed like a Yenching student I could almost certainly get him through. Actually, the Japanese sentry looked at us rather curiously but the motorcycle had very good acceleration and I reckoned that I would have been far enough away had he started shooting. Later we learnt that the man was Wang Yu, head of enemy area intelligence in Chin-Ch'a-Chi.

Another episode was merely amusing. My wife and I started from her parent's home to visit friends in the British Embassy and coming out on to the main road from a small path we found that, every hundred yards or so, a Japanese soldier with fixed bayonet was facing out into the countryside and we soon caught up with a convoy of several large cars followed by one lorry with Japanese soldiers and another with Chinese police. (Presumably some very high ranking Japanese had been taken to see the Summer Palace.) When we tried to pass, the Chinese police waved rifles at us so we fell back a few hundred yards and just short of the gate a Japanese gendarme with a pistol jumped out in front but only held us up for two or three minutes. When we got through the gates we found the streets completely cleared and were able to drive through Peking at about seventy miles an hour — every side road was blocked by Japanese soldiers and Chinese police.

For the last few months of 1941 most people in Peking were expecting war to start between Japan and the United States and I thought it would be a good idea to have a British team in Chin-Ch'a-Chi sending intelligence information to the British army. My friend, Captain Hill, who represented British military intelligence in Peking fully agreed and proposed to send his signals officer and I got a message through to General Nieh Jung-chen who gave his approval. However, the War Office kept on asking silly questions such as whether we really knew that there was a Chinese held area where a British team could operate — so the opportunity was lost. In fact the allies only started to get intelligence from the Communist held areas after the U.S. Army Observer's Section had arrived in Yenan in July 1944. Much earlier information from the main frontline area adjoining Manchuria might have made an appreciable difference to the course of history. One of the factors which induced the Western powers to make far reaching concessions at Yalta to secure Soviet participation against Japan was a belief that the Kuantung Army in Manchuria was so strong that it might carry on independent resistance even after the invasion of Japan. Better information about the Japanese order of battle would have revealed that the Kuantung Army had been reduced to third rate reservists whom the Russians were able to defeat completely in some ten days of fighting.

Dr. Stuart's plans to move Yenching to Chengtu were under way and he asked me to call a meeting of the foreign faculty to see who might be willing to get out through Chin-Ch'a-Chi. However, almost no one was interested. Miss Boring of the Biology Department said that she had made one trip into the countryside in winter and the water in the teapot had been frozen in the morning. General opinion was that the United States would be able to defeat Japan in a few months and that a short internment was preferable to facing the discomforts of the Chinese countryside in winter. The only people who wanted to leave were Professor William Band of the Physics Department, his wife Claire, and Rudolf Loewenthal, a Jewish refugee in the Department of Journalism.

Escape, December 1941.

I had expected that the Americans would be able to put off the actual outbreak of war until the marines were out of China. I had an appointment with the dentist on the Tuesday and was planning to leave on the Wednesday or Thursday. On the morning of Monday 8th December 1941 my wife got up to listen to the Chinese language news from the British station in Shanghai, could not get it and called me out of bed and I managed to hear the German station in Shanghai saying that a state of war existed between Japan and America. I was ready to try and shoot our way out; several Chinese friends had left pistols with me for safe keeping. However, our cook appeared and said that there were no Japanese at the gates ·of the campus, so I hastily took the President's car, picked up the Bands and some suitcases of wireless parts and went out from the back gate. (Rudolf Loewenthal could not be reached as he had an early morning class.) We abandoned the car short of the Japanese post at Wench'uan and walked off into the countryside, hiring a couple of farmers to carry our luggage concealed in their deep harvest baskets. We headed for the holiday house of a French doctor who had treated wounded Chinese soldiers but the man in charge, afraid to take us in, passed us on to another foreigner's house further into the hills. Here we were put in touch with a man who was nominally a village head under the Japanese regime but actually worked for the Communists. He hid us in a small Dragon Spring temple and the next night a man appeared whom I had met before when handing over supplies. He guided us round Miao Feng Shan and next morning we met the first Chinese troops.

The first Chinese troops we met in December 1941. On *k'ang*, Mrs. Band, Hsiao Li, Michael Lindsay.

Later we heard that the Kempetai had come to our house only ten minutes after our escape. Not apparently realizing how we had gone they spent several days questioning all our friends and warned that it would be a very serious offence to hide us. We still had Japanese blockade lines to cross before reaching the main base area and were forced to wait more than two weeks to accompany a party of troops. All the main villages had been destroyed and we were billeted with a family living in the small huts they had originally built to use while cultivating their fields in a small side valley. Certain equipment I had sent out from Peking was still in the area and we were able to assemble a receiver on which we heard the disastrous course of the war. I now realized that I had brought my razor but no razor blades, my pipe but no·tobacco and had left the collar off my shirt. Hsiao Li had left behind her jewellery and the money she had been keeping for just such an emergency. With nothing to do we slept about fourteen hours a day and I had a severe bout of fever.

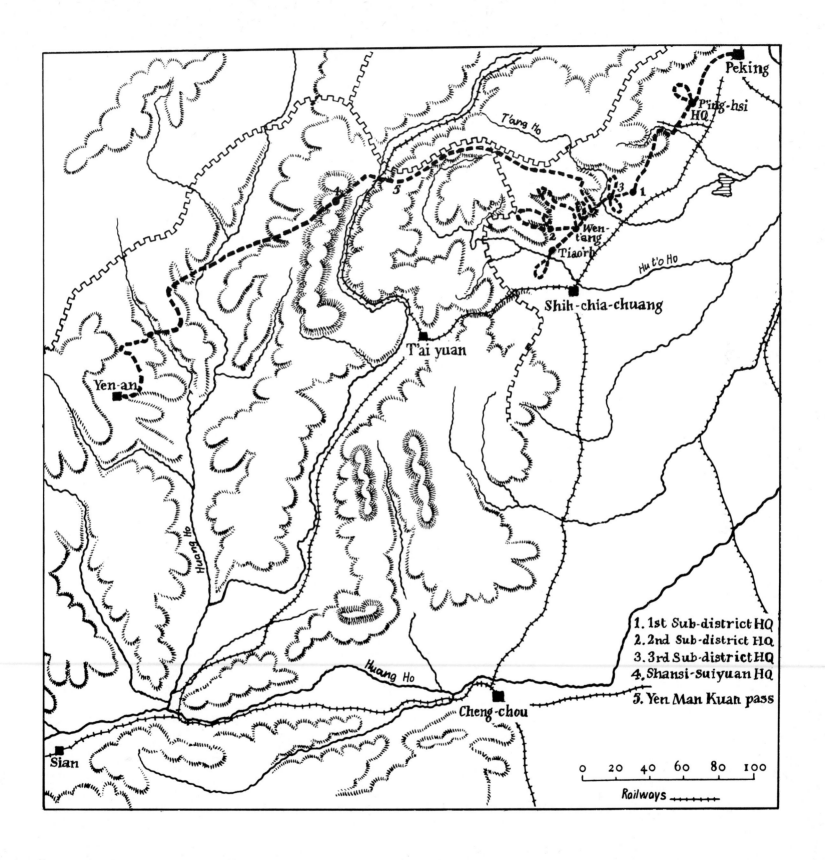

Peking

P'ing-hsi
HQ

T'ang Ho

3 1

Wen-
t'ang

2

Tiaorh

Hu t'o Ho

Shih-chia-chuang

T'ai yuan

Yen-an

Huang Ho

Huang Ho

Cheng-chou

Sian

1. 1st Sub-district HQ
2. 2nd Sub-district HQ
3. 3rd Sub-district HQ
4. Shansi-suiyuan HQ
5. Yen Man Kuan pass

0   20   40   60   80   100

Railways ╫╫╫╫╫

Pass going south from Pei Chu Ma Ho valley.

Old-style Chinese acupuncture.

Hsiao Li with peasant family.

Crossing Yun Ting river.

Peasant family with whom we stayed.

Small mountain village in P'inghsi.

Small hut where we stayed shortly after escape from Peking.

P'inghsi, January — March 1942.

General and Mrs. Hsiao K'e, P'inghsi. Mrs. Hsiao K'e and Mrs. Ho Lung were two very beautiful sisters who married two Red Army generals.

We finally reached General Hsiao K'e's Headquarters on New Year's Day, 1942, and stayed there some three months becoming good friends with Hsiao K'e and his wife. Hsiao Li was surprised to find him such a kind and scholarly man. He had been associated with General Ho Lung and, during the civil war, children had been told about Chu, Mao (Chu Te and Mao Tse-tung) and Ho Lung and had thought of them as fierce monsters with long teeth and red eyelids because the sound "Chu Mao" can mean pig's hair and "Ho Lung" river dragon.

We also met Wang Yu, the man whom I had taken into Peking on my motorcycle. He was stationed in a village some five miles away and we several times went over to talk to him. The communications section was in a village close by and I started helping them with their work; I had brought with me a test meter and a slide rule which turned out to be the only ones in the base area.

After the journey life at headquarters was relatively easy, we were able to get the lice out of our clothes and were provided with padded winter uniforms; even so, conditions were primitive. The ceilings were of paper pasted onto *kao-liang* stalks and at night mice would run over them eating the paste — one even fell through on to somebody's face. Food there was good and we certainly lived in far greater comfort than the foreigners later interned at Weihsien. At a feast given at local government headquarters I had the most delicious Chinese meal I have ever tasted. The cook had worked in one of Peking's most famous restaurants and there were at least fifteen dishes including local wild pheasant cooked in six or seven ways. The civilian government always seemed to have the best cooks. Another day, at headquarters, our dinner tasted like very tender stewed mutton and no-one could make out what it was until Hsiao K'e sent for the cook who, delighted we could not guess, explained that we had eaten the dog he had been fattening round the kitchen.

During our stay in P'inghsi three other foreigners appeared who had escaped from Peking. The first two were a Dutch engineer, Mr. Brondgeest, who had worked for the Peking Electricity

Rag paper making in small mountain village, Hsiao F'eng Ku. This is interesting as showing the extent to which even remote country areas could be self sufficient. The paper was rough but, thirty years later, has not deteriorated like wood pulp paper.

Company, and the son of a French official from the Customs Service, M. D'Anjou. A welcoming feast was given which included fried eggs covered with sugar, both scarce items at the time. The cook was anxious to know how the foreign friends had enjoyed his meal and my wife told him they had thought it extremely good except for the eggs with sugar. He thought this very strange, knowing that foreigners liked eggs and that compared with the Chinese they had a very sweet tooth he was sure that fried eggs with sugar would be especially attractive.

The next arrival was an Austrian refugee, Dr. Frey. He was about six foot three with correspondingly large feet; his boots were beginning to disintegrate and the chief of staff got a drawing of his foot and sent it to the supply department to have some Chinese shoes made. However, the local workers declared that it was impossible for anyone to have feet so large and refused to make them. Later, when we had arrived in 1st. sub-district, people were determined to get shoes large enough and sent a drawing made round the outside of his boots, which resulted in a pair nearly eighteen inches long. A third try did produce wearable shoes. The regular Chinese shoes were made entirely of cloth and peasants would turn their clothing into shoes when it became too ragged. The soles were layers of cloth sewn together to a thickness of about half an inch, and winter shoes had the uppers padded for warmth. Of course these were not at all waterproof but this was no problem as it was very seldom wet except in summer.

Meeting at Hsiao K'e's Headquarters.

To 1st. sub-district, April 1942.

We left P'inghsi for 1st. sub-district in the spring. The journey involved crossing one Japanese held motor road but was reasonably uneventful. Given that there were no roads, travel arrangements in the base area were good. On the more regularly travelled routes there were places where travellers on official business could stay, and we particularly liked passing through Wen-t'ang, (Hot Pool), where there were two bathing pools, one for men and one for women, with sulphur water so hot that one had to submerge very gradually, and it completely cured my scabies. The only disadvantages there came from the man in charge who illustrated the disadvantages of old-fashioned Chinese courtesy. On our first visit our evening meal consisted of *lao-ping*, fried wheat cakes, a common peasant food. He was most apologetic and said that for breakfast he would give me *lao-ping* with eggs in them. He would not believe me when I told him that I liked *lao-ping* and thought that they would not be at all good with eggs in them, and when he produced them for breakfast I only ate them out of politeness. On another occasion in winter he refused to believe people who told him that their *k'ang* was quite warm enough and insisted on burning more wood; in the middle of the night, the mat and bedding started to smoulder.

Arrangements for feeding troops on the move were excellent. Taxation was payable mainly in grain and each village was responsible for delivering its tax grain to a local depot if it had not been issued locally. The supply officer of any unit on the move carried "grain tickets" issued in multiples of half a day's ration — eleven ounces. In any village he could go to the village council and get food; and the villagers preferred this because they could deliver bits of paper to account for their taxes instead of transporting grain. The system had improved between 1939 and 1942. In 1939 some villagers had complained about delivering grain to inconveniently distant points and sometimes had long delays in getting repaid by the government. The need for repayments arose when the demand of large concentrations of troops exceeded the local taxes. Supply department officials then had to negotiate for the loan of grain beyond the tax quota.

The supply department was extremely efficient and when I was asked to look at the system I could not suggest any improvements. Their book-keeping was regular double-entry in which one could get out trial balances for grain and for money, and they insisted on strict adherence to their rules. Except during a Japanese offensive when all units were issued with a supply of grain tickets, every unit had to turn in its account for the past month before they could get their ration issue for the next. What was really remarkable was the ability of the supply department to function even during an offensive. In the middle of a long Japanese offensive in the main base area which went on from mid-September to late December 1943, and with Japanese troops everywhere, the supply department issued everyone with winter uniforms. We got ours as soon as

Meeting at 1st. sub-district.

the weather started to get cold and other people who had been in quite different parts of the area reported the same experience.

In most places winter uniforms consisted of a khaki cotton padded tunic, cotton padded trousers and a cotton padded overcoat. These were very warm except in strong winds. In 2nd. sub-district and at Yenan, where the climate was much colder and the winds stronger, tunic, trousers and overcoat had sheepskin with the fur inwards between the outer cotton and the lining. Uniforms had no badges of rank but officers' uniforms were visibly better made, where sheepskin was used, had long-haired lambskin, and the lining was of silk. I still have my Yenan winter uniform and find it very useful in freezing weather. Yenan differed from the front line areas in keeping the old Chinese army dark blue-grey instead of khaki.

People in the army and government organisations were on a supply system with salaries being merely pocket money. We spent ours on buying things like tobacco leaves and fruit — persimmons in winter, peaches, pears and small Chinese dates in summer. After we had returned to England the Inland Revenue asked me about my income for the previous years, but they gave up when I produced a figure in *chin* of millet per month. The supply system and the taxation in grain were important in insulating the whole public sector from the effects of inflation. The Chin-Ch'a-Chi currency had depreciated though not so badly as the National Government currency. (In 1944 when I met people who had come from Chungking and asked about prices of commodities common to both areas the purchasing power of a Chin-Ch'a-Chi dollar seemed equal to about four National Government dollars.) In National Government areas the effects of inflation were disastrous producing a situation in which even officials who wanted to be honest could not live on their salaries. In the Communist areas with the main accounting system based on grain the depreciation of money had little effect on the public sector, and the private sector of the economy was mainly subsistence agriculture.

Returning to the spring of 1942, we moved on to General Nieh Jung-chen's Headquarters visiting various organisations on the way. General Nieh had heard of my work for the P'inghsi communications department and asked if I would stay on as technical adviser to the army communications department in his area.

Tiao'rh, May — October 1942.

Until October that year we lived in the village of Tiao'rh in a side valley running north from the Fu To River, General Nieh's Headquarters was four or five miles to the north and the main army communications department in a village about a mile to the south.

I gave classes in radio engineering to the army technicians and as we had very few text books a great deal had to be worked out from the first principles of electrical theory. We were asked to produce a more sensitive and selective receiver for communications with the very low power station in the Hopei-Liaoning area and decided to build a superheterodyne. To get the formula for proper tracking requires the solution of three simultaneous cubic equations and all the mathematical talent of the area was put on to the job. Later we acquired a copy of Terman's *Radio Engineering* — and found that our formula gave the right result though it was awkward to use because it involved small differences between large numbers so the calculation could not be done on a slide rule. Visiting the People's Republic in 1973 I was pleased to find that people who had taken my courses in Chin-Ch'a-Chi held a high proportion of the top positions in telecommunications.

I also started a general rebuilding of equipment. The old transmitters were plain Hartley oscillators in large boxes, about two foot square by one. We rebuilt these with a master oscillator-power amplifier circuit and logarithmic tappings on the output coil to adjust the loading. The new sets had much better frequency stability and could be fitted into a box of about ten by eight by six inches though it was seldom possible to build two sets exactly the same. Some components came from captured Japanese equipment but most were smuggled out from Japanese occupied cities by merchants who would take the risk for sufficiently high prices.

Receivers consisted of an oscillating detector with two transformer coupled audio stages, and for these, in most cases, we did not change the circuit but rebuilt them much smaller. Receivers were battery operated and most transmitters got their power from a hand generator — no better power sources were available in Chin-Ch'a-Chi. Our best transmitters had an output power of about twenty-five watts and as the typical station had to operate both over fairly short distances and over ranges of several hundred miles we tried to make our sets with a frequency range from 10 MHz. to 2.5 MHz.

Later, at Yenan, when the Americans proposed giving us equipment for a network transmitting the information they needed from the front line I discovered that the American army did not have any sets which met our needs. American hand generators were better and lighter than ours but their idea of portable equipment was something which could be carried in a jeep. All sets had a main unit weighing over forty pounds and also had frequency ranges of only about 3:2 against our 4:1.

Hsiao Li was also working for the communications department giving classes in English because simple English was used for service messages — Chinese characters can only be sent as four figure groups. Really skilled operators know nearly all the nine thousand odd groups for the characters in standard telegraph code; I have seen operators listening to four figure groups and writing down characters. However, ordinary army operators would have had to spend hours with the telegraph code book for even basic service messages and learning a little English was far

Old radio equipment.

New type equipment.

more convenient. I was told that it took at least five years to train an expert operator to go between four figure groups and characters without continual reference to the code book. Telegrams in Chinese also have very little redundancy. In an alphabetic language a single error need only produce a misspelling without changing the sense. In Chinese it always produces a different character. I heard an amusing story about this in the New China News Agency at Yenan. In one speech Mao Tse-tung had used a four character phrase "from masses win respect", which was received in Southeast Shansi with two figures wrong out of the sixteen which turned it into "from fog win treasure". The editors of the local newspaper did not deduce that this must be garbled but wrote an editorial explaining the deep inner meaning of winning a treasure from the fog. When the *Chin Tung Nan Jih Pao* reached Yenan months later the editorial caused some bewilderment until its basis was discovered.

I had nothing to do with the coding of messages but learnt much later that this was another important field of Communist efficiency. In Japan in 1967 I met a man who had worked on monitoring enemy traffic during the war, who told me that it was only in February 1941 that the Japanese cryptographers managed to break the Communist code. For nearly a year the Japanese could read Communist messages; and it was a year in which the Communist armies did rather badly. However, they changed their code which the Japanese still had not broken by the end of the war. By contrast, National Government codes were poor and the Japanese could read their messages throughout the war.

Certain aspects of the Chinese Communist war time organisation were inefficient but the Communists did seem able to allot competent personnel to really vital work — such as in the army supply department and message coding.

At Tiao'rh all foreigners lived in a courtyard we called the "International Hotel". Dr. Frey soon left to work in the hospital but we had other arrivals, the first a very eccentric Frenchman, Mr. Ullman, who turned up in a naval officer's uniform. He had returned to Peking after the French surrender and after a spell in the navy as a reservist. He had had no difficulty in escaping from Peking as he had simply walked out explaining to the Japanese sentries that he had been crossed in love, which was true, and was retiring to a temple in the hills to meditate. He brought with him a few books on Buddhism and Schopenhauer's *Aphorismen zur Lebensweisheit,* and covered the walls of his room with poems to the lady who had rejected him.

Michael Lindsay giving Radio Engineering course.

Next to appear were the manager of the Peking branch of the National City Bank, Mr. G. M. Hall, with a German girl, Miss Brennecke. She was engaged to an American working for an oil company in Chungking but had not married him because American wives were being sent home. While alone in Shanghai she was trapped by the Pacific war. Determined to return to her fiancé she somehow managed to contact the Chinese underground in Shanghai who told her it was easier to get out from Peking. With her German passport she had no difficulty in travelling to Peking where the Communist organisation offered to arrange her journey if she would help in getting the American bank manager out of the city. They drove through the gate in an embassy car flying the German flag. She brought a huge load of luggage — many dresses, an electric iron and a large portrait of her fiancé in a silver frame. General Nieh firmly said he was not going to move all this across Japanese blockade lines and cut her down to what one man could carry. The local army drama troupe was glad to acquire a selection of western clothes.

Mr. Hall was like Dr. Bethune in being quite unable to learn Chinese. Having nothing else to do, he spent several hours a day taking lessons from Hsiao Li but simply could not distinguish the words. She was astonished when he asked if we had killed many apricots in our room — he had mixed up *hsing erh* (apricot) and *hsieh tze* (scorpion).

Lindsays at Tiao'rh.

At Tiao'rh. Hsiao Li, Michael Lindsay, ?, Liu K'e (manager of "International Hotel"), Mr. Hall, Miss Brennecke.

1942 was relatively peaceful. There had been a big Japanese offensive in 1941 but during 1942 they concentrated on other areas. We had to move out for a few days during a minor raid, and once a Japanese plane strafed the valley killing several civilians but this was an isolated episode. The Japanese made surprisingly little use of their air power.

We attended a number of mass meetings and drama performances and went to 4th sub-district Headquarters south of the Fu To river for a celebration of Red Army day on August 1st.

Mass meeting near Tiao'rh.

By October conditions for crossing the T'aiyuan-Tat'ung railway improved and the foreign community at Tiao'rh dispersed. Brondgeest, d'Anjou and Ullman left first and were soon followed by Mr. Hall and Miss Brennecke. Foreign behaviour continued to be eccentric. When Hsiao Li and I reached 2nd. sub-district Headquarters in 1943 the general, chief of staff and political officer were pleased to meet a foreigner who behaved in a normal way. The chief of staff remarked that if my eyes had been the right colour and my nose a bit smaller I might really have been Chinese. While Brondgeest, d'Anjou and Ullman were waiting to set off across the railway, Brondgeest caught a baby sparrow and tamed it as a pet. Ullman was jealous and wrote a long letter in Chinese to the political officer asking the army political department to produce a pet sparrow for him.

Hsiao Li and I were expecting our first child and the army medical department had prepared rooms for her and Mrs. Sung Shao-wan who was also expecting a baby. (Sung Shao-wan was chairman of the government.) However, on the night Hsaio Li reached the medical department there was a Japanese raid up the Sha river valley and she had to move to a very remote small village in the high mountains over a ridge called the King of Hell's Nose. This village was so isolated that some of the men still wore their hair in a pigtail not knowing that the Emperor had been deposed thirty years before. An expert obstetrician who had worked in the Peking Union Medical College luckily reached the village just before our daughter was born. Mrs. Sung's baby arrived a few days later and after a week they were able to move down again to the medical department village where I could join them.

I had decided that the best way to handle the rebuilding of apparatus was for me to travel round to the various sub-district headquarters. One of the satisfactory things about work in Chin-Ch'a-Chi was that one could always get support if one could make

Old man burying possessions in ruins on news of Japanese approach.

a good case for some suggestion. This travelling round to rebuild apparatus was one example. More important was the pooling of supplies. I discovered that various organisations had been hoarding components, and when one of my students mentioned that the important Party organisation he had come from had a large stock of valves — a very scarce item — I wrote a memorandum arguing that we could build a good many more sets if all components in the area were made available to the central communications department. This produced an order from General Nieh that all components should be reported and made available.

Staying in various sub-district headquarters we could observe the working of the army system. Certain foreign writers have argued that there was frequent friction between the regular army officers and the political officers but we did not notice this. The general, the chief of staff and the political officer seemed everywhere to be a harmonious three-man team. As we ate with the headquarters staff and often sat round talking with them in the evenings any bad feelings would almost certainly have been noticeable to Hsiao Li who is sensitive to nuances in Chinese behaviour.

We could also observe the working of the intelligence system. At set hours in the afternoon, the chief of staff would receive reports of all Japanese movements. Peasants working near Japanese forts would report any increase or decrease in their garrisons or any movements of supplies, and nearby Chinese army units would pass on these reports by wireless or telephone. The result was that the Japanese were never able to make a surprise attack except on a very small scale. For any serious offensive they needed to concentrate troops and build up supplies and this would give us at least a week's notice to hide or bury our own supplies and prepare to move.

The lines of the telephone system were galvanized iron wire on wooden posts and followed the ridges rather than the valleys for greater security against Japanese raids. Except in wet weather they gave reasonable communication over about forty miles for telephony and longer distances for telegraphy. We attempted to make repeater units but could not produce satisfactorily balanced and shielded transformers.

By contrast, Japanese intelligence about the Chinese forces was very poor. During their 1943 offensive we captured a Japanese map dated the beginning of September, just before the offensive started. This had most things wrong. General Nieh's Headquarters was shown at a village from which he had moved in April and the communications department centre was put at 1st. sub-district Headquarters. I think I know the source of this last error. While I was working at 1st. sub-district a merchant appeared with a stock of batteries and other supplies and we were later told that he was a Japanese agent and must have reported the activity in rebuilding equipment.

Red Army Day.

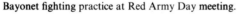

Bayonet fighting practice at Red Army Day meeting.

Grenade throwing practice.

Back to 1st. sub-district, November 1942.

Hsiao Li and I travelled with our baby, Erica, to 1st. sub-district, General Yang Ch'eng-wu's Headquarters, where I was laid up for several days with very bad toothache; luckily, the one dentist in the area was close at hand and came to extract the infected tooth.

The defection of the head of Yang Ch'eng-wu's communications section was the one case I heard of where someone went over from the Communists to the Japanese. He had seduced the daughter of the family with whom he was billeted and had peculated over buying supplies. Knowing he would be in serious trouble he ran away to the Japanese and later the army sent plain clothes agents to assassinate him in I-hsien city. In 1949, going through the files of a Japanese controlled newspaper in Peking, I found other reports of Communist desertions and surrenders; all were on a very small scale and may have been captures rather than desertions.

Lang Ya Shan (Wolf's Tooth Mountains) near 1st. sub-district Headquarters taken after one of the rare winter snowfalls. On the top a memorial had been erected for soldiers who had defended Lang Ya Shan against a Japanese attack until ammunition had run out. The defence and the escape of the survivors was helped by a Taoist hermit who lived in a temple near the top of the mountain.

Taoist hermit.

We came across one interesting instance of this when we met a man, Chu Chan-k'uei, who had been a sub-district commander in Central Hopei. He had been captured in late 1941 by the Japanese who tried very hard to persuade him to work for them because he was a native of North China, unlike most of the higher Communist officers who had started with the Red Army in South or Central China. Finally they told him that, whether he liked it or not, they would announce his appointment as commander of a Chinese division at Shih-chia-chuang. He managed to jump off the train carrying him there from Peking and make his way back to the Chin-Ch'a-Chi base area. While held in Peking, Japanese officers talked fairly freely about their plans. They told him that the Germans were trying to persuade them to attack India and the Soviet Union but they did not want to do either until they had captured Australia. The capture of Australia would deprive the Americans of any suitable base for a counter-offensive and would give them a supply of the wool they needed for winter uniforms in a Siberian campaign.

Staff of medical school.

These reports of Japanese army thinking raise interesting possible alternatives for history. If the Japanese had attacked India immediately after their conquest of Burma, instead of waiting until 1944, the British position might have collapsed. If they had attacked the Soviet Union at the time of maximum German penetration the Soviet position would have been seriously weakened.

3rd. sub-district, January — February 1943.

We stayed at 1st. sub-district until January 1943 and then went on, first to 3rd. sub-district Headquarters under General Huang Yung-sheng, and then to the Headquarters of General Lü Chang-ts'ao whose troops were starting to filter back into Central Hopei. These two headquarters were close to each other and near the Medical School and we became friends with Chiang I-chen, the head of the army medical department and formerly Dr. Bethune's chief assistant. He had had a most fascinating career. A native of Fukien, he had joined the Red Army as a small boy, had been attached as part servant, part apprentice to a captured National Government army doctor and learnt a good deal more from Dr. Bethune. Without any regular medical training he had become an extremely expert surgeon and could remove an appendix in roughly half the time taken by Dr. Kotnis, an Indian sent by the Congress Party, who worked in the medical school until he died of cerebral malaria in 1942. Chiang I-chen was also renowned for his extremely strong head for drink and for the skill with which he could cheat at Mah-jong.

Meal time at medical school.

When the Medical School was to move to another area General Huang Yung-sheng gave a farewell banquet for Chiang I-chen and his staff, determined that this time at least they would make him drunk. The next morning Dr. Ch'en, the number two at the school, told us of his disturbed night. About midnight General Huang had

Erica with Chiang I-chen (centre).

General Lü Cheng ts'ao and family.

telephoned to say that Chiang I-chen had become unconscious and Dr. Ch'en advised that he should be left to sleep it off. Twice more during the night there were calls to say that he was still unconscious but Dr. Ch'en could only repeat his advice. In fact, Chiang recovered the next day but I asked Dr. Ch'en how they would have announced it if he had died; they could hardly have reported, as in the standard form for deaths in action, that he had "nobly sacrificed his life."

Old Red Army men like Chiang I-chen were usually far more independent than the newer recruits to the Communist organisation. These recruits, mostly students from Peking or Tientsin, felt that they had a bourgeois background to live down and any disagreement they might have with an official Party pronouncement could only come from their failure to eliminate influences from this bad background. Those who had spent all their active life in the Communist organisation felt that there was no possible doubt that they were good Communists and that, if they thought some official Party pronouncement was not sensible, perhaps this was really so. At one time there was a Central Committee directive that all areas should try to increase their degree of self sufficiency and the army medical department was ordered to cut down on its purchases of drugs smuggled from the Japanese occupied cities and step up its production of locally made medicines. Chiang I-chen protested, pointing out that locally made drugs were extremely expensive in terms of the labour needed to produce them and were also much less effective than imported drugs. His argument was accepted and he was actually congratulated for having made his protest.

It was also noticeable that people whose experience had been entirely at base Headquarters tended to be much more doctrinaire than people with experience at the front. While staying at Lü Cheng-ts'ao's Headquarters, I was lent a little book by Mao Tse-tung on dialectical materialism. It seemed to make better sense than other books I had read on the subject and when a man called Chou Hsiao-chou who had recently come from Yenan to join the political department asked me what I thought of it, I replied that I thought it rather good and that, in the chapter on dialectical materialism and science and mathematics, what Mao said agreed with what had been said by non-Marxist writers on the philosophy of science. I mentioned one passage which was rather like Einstein's saying that, in so far as mathematical theorems were exactly true they did not apply to the real world and that, in so far as they applied to the real world, they were not exactly true. Chou Hsiao-chou was shocked by the idea that Mao could be in agreement with non-Marxists and we argued all one evening until I reduced him to saying that the same proposition could be true when asserted by a Marxist and false when asserted by a non-Marxist. People who had been listening told me next day that Chou was an extremely doctrinaire man and they were pleased I had shown him to be talking nonsense.

The book itself is an interesting subject. When we visited China in 1949 I asked several friends in the Party if they could get a copy for me. They did not deny its existence but could not get one. (A book printed at Yenan before 1943 might well have been unavailable in 1949.) However, in the 1960's Edgar Snow published an interview with Mao Tse-tung in which Mao asserted that he had never produced such a book. It is likely that a book which tried to make sense out of dialectical materialism was unorthodox Marxist-Leninism and that, when Mao had realised this, he wanted to repudiate his work. Up to 1949 the Communists followed the Chinese tradition of respect for historical documents but the editions of Mao's works published after 1951 omit or change passages where he regretted what he had actually written — for example, the passage from *New Democracy,* (1940), in which he wrote that an alliance between China and Britain and the United States could only be directed against the Soviet Union and not against Japan.

Trying out locally made copy of small Japanese mortar. Dr. Frey firing it.

Mass meeting at 3rd. sub-district.

Preliminary story telling before drama performance, 3rd. sub-district.

Chung Pai Ch'a, May — September 1943.

On returning to central Headquarters we found Nieh Jung-chen had moved to Wen-t'ang and that the communications department was now in the village of Chung Pai Ch'a about four miles away. It was a poor place with few fields and in spring before the winter wheat was harvested everyone was reduced to eating an unpalatable soup made of poplar leaves. A large hall had been built at Wen-t'ang for the meeting of the Chin-Ch'a-Chi regional congress held in January 1943, but in April or May the Japanese bombed this to ruins. The bombing was confined to Wen-t'ang but the planes passed so low over Chen Pai Ch'a we were forced to take refuge in a small ravine.

Professor and Mrs. Band now decided to leave for Yenan and Chungkung and Dr. Frey and I were the only foreigners left. Some time in 1942 all allied nationals in North China had been interned at Weihsien in Shantung so no more could escape into Chin-Ch'a-Chi, but one day we were surprised to hear that an Englishman and an American had arrived at Headquarters, and we went over to see them. They were extremely frightened to see us. The alleged Englishman, who called himself Hawkins, could hardly speak English and they were in fact White Russians who had got into trouble with the Japanese authorities in Peking and had been offered a pardon if they could bring intelligence from the Communist areas. They had been safe as long as no one spoke

Stilt dance celebrating Chinese New Year.

English but at Nieh's Headquarters they encountered not only us but also Chao Ming the Yenching student who had travelled with me in 1939 and was now with the Public Safety Bureau. They were later shot as spies.

I wasted a lot of time in the spring of 1943 trying to establish contact with British Intelligence in Chungking. Before Mr. Hall left in October 1942, I had borrowed Dr. Bethune's typewriter, the only one in the area, and had written a long report which I asked him to give to British Intelligence and, if possible, to publish. Also, with General Nieh's approval, I had suggested plans for wireless contacts, allowing about six months for Mr. Hall to reach Chungking and make the necessary arrangements. After we had no reply to our calls for several weeks I discovered the call sign of Chou En-lai's station in Chungking and made contact but they refused to pass on any message for fear of trouble with the National Government, which did close down the station in 1944. When the Americans came to Yenan I learnt the true story. American Headquarters at Chungking had entrusted the contact to a station manned by operatives from Tai Li's organisation, the very organisation responsible for maintaining the blockade of the Communist areas. This shows General Stilwell's extraordinary naiveté in some respects. The Americans also classified my report and did not pass it on to the British though it was finally published in 1945 when John Service gave it to *Amerasia*.

I heard much later that Mr. Hall's reports had had considerable influence. By 1943 the National Government was maintaining that the Communists were not fighting the Japanese and that Hopei was entirely under Japanese occupation. Mr. Hall's reports to the contrary carried conviction — a Republican bank manager was hardly likely to be a Communist propagandist.

Chung Pai Ch'a.

Hall built for meeting of Chin-Ch'a-Chi Congress in January 1943. Bombed in April 1943.

Until September we lived peacefully at Chung Pai Ch'a with occasional trips for meetings or celebrations. We acquired a delightful pet when one of my students gave me a very small chipmunk whose mother had run away. As he grew bigger we gave him the run of the house and though he often went out for the day always came home at night, and he loved to play with Erica who was just starting to crawl. Hsiao Li also acquired some leghorn hens which the Agriculture Department were introducing to the area.

By early September we had warnings that the Japanese were preparing a major offensive. The radio department hid all its equipment and when the offensive started in the middle of the month, we moved into the high mountains staying for a week or so in a very small village of four or five thatched houses called Hsi Mu Ch'iao (West Wooden Bridge) though there was no bridge and a stream so narrow one could step over it.

Hsi Mu Ch'iao.

Lindsay family on march.

On the move, September — December 1943.

We then moved on to 2nd. sub-district and were stationed with a scouting company at the slightly less primitive village of Mu Ch'ang. With nothing else to do we helped some people who were harvesting pumpkins and corn in nearby fields. They turned out to be a local landlord family and brought us a welcome present of fresh vegetables — pumpkins, turnips, cabbage, leeks and even some green beans.

With Scouting Company.

A hawk appeared in the village and was identified as coming from a village in Wu T'ai. Apparently such hawks could be used until the owner came to reclaim them and the local expert took the hawk and I went along with the hunting party; it was very strenuous exercise. Once the hawk had been released at a pheasant we had to race over the steep mountain to catch it before it had eaten its prey and become uninterested in further sport.

One episode there showed the reality of the Communist army claim to respect civilian property. The scouting company had some flour and wanted to make *mien pien'rh* — strips of dough rolled out and boiled. This required a rolling pin and the only one in the village belonged to an old woman who having just bought it at a high price refused to lend it. The soldiers were quite prepared to accept her refusal but Hsiao Li talked the old woman into lending her the rolling pin as a special favour. Having lived in the country as a girl she found it easier to get on good terms with the peasant women than the official organisers of the women's mass movement. In this area she could also speak something near to the local dialect.

After a few weeks the Japanese approached Mu Ch'ang. We had good warning of this but there was a misunderstanding over the telephone. 2nd. sub-district Headquarters later told us that they had instructed the scouting company to move with us to guard us. The scouting company understood that we were to remain with them and, as a scouting company, it was their duty to remain close to the enemy. A Japanese plane flew over the village dropping leaflets promising good treatment to those who did not resist and we soon heard firing further down the valley. The officer in charge sent us with one soldier as guide into a small side valley to the south where we waited for several hours and finally heard the

Militia mining village as Japanese approach, 2nd. sub-district.

sound of firing and hand grenades from near Mu Ch'ang. Our guide wanted to go to another very small village to find porters for our luggage but I said we had better abandon it and get out. We left our stock of rice and Lao Wang's big cooking chopper but he insisted on carrying his basic equipment. Wang Ch'eng-liang only carried Erica, the nurse carried Erica's napkins and dried biscuit, Hsiao Li carried our little radio and I carried my test meter and slide rule and basic necessities like our washing things. We went up the valley and, on the pass at the top, met an army drama company coming the other way. Their leader asked our guide whether they had time to cross the main valley, and while they were discussing this, soldiers from the scouting company who had moved towards the pass up another side valley started firing at the Japanese a hundred yards away; about ten were killed in the engagement.

Everyone rushed down from the pass to the south and our guide took us eastwards into the mountains, delivering us late at night to a small village which the Japanese had never penetrated. This place, though small, was rich and still had paraffin for lamps, though nearly everywhere else had gone back to vegetable oil. At dawn as we moved out onto the mountain tops, we heard artillery fire and saw wolves along the skyline. We returned to the same village after dark, and having lost touch with the organisation and hearing no news of Japanese movements our guide advised moving out before dawn the next day. We climbed down a very small and steep track and after half an hour's walk a man came running after us to report that the Japanese had moved on the village at dawn by every path except the one we had taken.

Later that day we re-established contact. In fact, it was not safe to move in the larger valleys without a guide from the local militia to point out where the paths were mined.

We met one section from 2nd. sub-district Headquarters who sent us off to join a party of other non-combatants who were moving out. Luckily we missed them because this party was ambushed by the Japanese and most people in it, including the children, killed. Our guide then decided to try and rejoin the scouting company. In the afternoon we came to a deserted village, discovering in one house a meal prepared but left uneaten; we were hungry and finished it off. Shots were fired but our guide thought he recognized the sound as that of Chinese rifles so we moved on and found that we had at last reached the scouting company.

We then moved to Shansi, passing through another deserted village surrounded by uncultivated fields, in a region the Japanese had declared a no-man's land where they would shoot anyone on sight, and people were living in small huts in the side valleys reached only by heavily mined paths.

2nd. sub-district, December 1943 — January 1944.

When we heard that the Japanese were retiring we moved to 2nd. sub-district Headquarters. Throughout all these moves Erica had slept peacefully. Most of the time she was carried, which made her wakeful at night and when she did sleep she lay with her arms wide out taking up far too much room when fifteen or twenty people might be trying to sleep on one *k'ang*.

We stayed there for several weeks while I worked on the rebuilding of their apparatus. We were surprised to find the village practically undamaged though the Japanese had been through there, and we were told that this was because of very effective use of land mines by the local militia. After the Japanese left more than thirty mines were found to have exploded round the edge. They must have decided it was too dangerous to venture into the village and had only burned one or two houses on the outskirts. The militia unit was congratulated at a big meeting to celebrate the end of the offensive and arrangements were made to send some of its members round to demonstrate their technique to other units.

We also saw something of a campaign to tighten up the enforcement of the rent reduction laws. We attended one meeting where the proceedings were rather like those of later people's courts in form though the substance was quite different because the landlord accused of over-charging was allowed to argue his case. On our first night's stop after leaving we met the landlord whom we had helped in his fields. He complained that the campaign was working unfairly, he had been convicted of charging too much rent and did not dispute this verdict but he had charged rent on what the land was assessed for tax and the actual harvest that year had been lower. Ordered to repay in grain which,

Mass meeting to celebrate end of Japanese offensive, 2nd. sub-district. Land mines as fireworks on opposite hillside.

at the end of the Japanese offensive was very scarce, he had offered his tenants land instead. Most had accepted but one or two insisted on repayment in grain and would only accept land at a ridiculously low valuation. Some weeks later we met the Standing Committee of the Regional Congress and told them about this case. The Communist member was inclined to say, "Hard cases make bad law." but the others agreed that the campaign seemed to be working unfairly and said they would send an investigating team to the area.

On our way back to central Headquarters we passed through Chung Pai Ch'a and found that the Japanese had burned the village, and both Central Headquarters and the communications department had moved to a valley north of the Sha River.

During 1943, relations between the Communists and the Kuomintang deteriorated badly. The National Government moved large forces under General Hu Tsung-nan to the area south of Yenan and the Communists countered this by moving General Ho Lung's troops to their side of the frontier. General Lü Cheng-ts'ao was transferred to Ho Lung's former base area in Shansi-Suiyan.

The house we lived in at **Chung Pai Ch'a** in January 1944 after Japanese offensive.

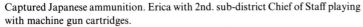

Captured Japanese ammunition. Erica with 2nd. sub-district Chief of Staff playing with machine gun cartridges.

Building caves for new Chin-Ch'a-Chi Headquarters (to make destruction by Japanese more difficult).

People's court in rent reduction campaign, 2nd. sub-district.

Head of army political department addressing meeting on sixth anniversary of setting up of Chin-Ch'a-Chi government.

Starting journey from Chin-Ch'a-Chi to Yenan.

1944.

Soon after we returned to central Headquarters at the beginning of 1944 I found that I had used up almost all available components for building new equipment and had taught almost all the army technicians with enough knowledge of mathematics to benefit. I felt very strongly that the complete isolation of the Communist areas, which could provide valuable intelligence, was seriously harming the allied war effort in China. It seemed that the most useful thing I could do would be to make fresh efforts to establish contacts with the British or American organisation in Chungking and that I would have more chance of doing this from Yenan than from Chin Ch'a-Chi. I therefore suggested to General Nieh that we should move to Yenan.

To Yenan, April — May 1944.

We left in early April with a training regiment that was going to Shensi-Kansu-Ninghsia. We first went northwest into very wild mountain country where the main crops were oats and potatoes. Most people in the party disliked oatmeal and potatoes but Hsiao Li and I were quite satisfied. Oatmeal had been a common food in her old home area and I had been brought up on porridge, and we felt that the only thing wrong with potatoes was that most Chinese did not realise how long they needed to be cooked.

We had to cross three Japanese lines. The first was a motor road in the upper Fu To River valley which brought us onto a ridge running south-west with traces of a branch of the Great Wall. Here it was nothing like the section at Nan-k'ou usually visited by tourists, there was only a mound seldom more than six feet high. Next we came to the pass over this ridge at Yen Men Kuan where a motor road was guarded by a Japanese fort, and finally we reached the most difficult crossing, the T'aiyuan-Tat'ung railway. Luckily, Commander Liu was an extremely able officer, very skilled at judging the probable actions of the Japanese and very strict about moving on time. The party following us had a less able commander and, on their first attempt only reached the railway at dawn where they encountered the Japanese and suffered casualties.

We set off at six one morning and marched till about three in the afternoon when we waited until night fell. It was raining and so dark that, at times, one had to hold on to the belt of the person in front to keep in line. Commander Liu had judged that the movements of his party, of some four hundred, would certainly have become known to the Japanese who would be expecting us to try to cross in the middle between two forts. He therefore crossed very close to one Japanese position, so near Ning-wu town that the railway track was lighted by the headlamp of a locomotive in the station. As morning came we were climbing up the snow covered hillside to the west and went on till after mid-day when we had a few hours rest but it was not until after dark that night that we reached somewhere safe enough to stop.

Northwest Shansi was very different country with a great deal

Commander Liu.

of fir forest cover remaining, and one could see very clearly the erosion produced by deforestation. Valleys where the forest remained on the hillsides had fairly narrow river channels with fields on either side, but in the bottom of the valleys where the forest had been destroyed there was gravel flood plain.

Commander Liu guessed that the Japanese might try to ambush our party on the track that led through the centre of a big forest and therefore took us round the edge close to a Japanese held city in the valley below. We heard afterwards that he had guessed right, and a party of Japanese had waited for nearly a week in the centre of the forest.

Finally we reached Shansi-Suiyuan Headquarters in a partially ruined *hsien* city. It was pleasant to meet Lü cheng-ts'ao again and Erica enjoyed playing with his baby who was about the same age, but after a week we had to move on once more. We had a hair-raising journey over ice-bound streams, and the only way the mules could cross was by spreading earth on the slippery surface.

We reached the Yellow River and were ferried over on large boats. On the west bank it was surprising to be in country that had not been fought over and where towns and villages were undamaged. On the second day we reached the city of Suiteh to be told that we had just missed a lorry going to Yenan and had to decide whether to wait for another which would do the one hundred and twenty miles to Yenan in a day or to go ahead on foot which might take a week.

After crossing T'aiyuan-Tat'ung railway.

Crossing Yellow River.

Journey from Shansi-Suiyuan Headquarters to Yellow River.

At this point I had my first experience of the inefficient organisation in Shansi-Kansu-Ninghsia. When we were introduced to the general in command at Suiteh I asked him if he could send a telegram to Yenan asking when another lorry would be likely to come. He replied that although he would be glad to do this it would be no use because people at Yenan did not answer telegrams; if he had any urgent business he sent a courier on horseback. Asked whether, if the Japanese started an attack across the Yellow River, he would only be able to get instructions by sending a courier, he replied that, of course they would answer that sort of telegram but Mao Tse-tung's desk was piled so high with messages from all the Communist areas that one could not expect him to answer an inquiry about the next lorry to Suiteh. My reaction was that if a telegram about the next lorry to Suiteh got on to Mao Tse-tung's desk, organisation at Yenan must be pretty inefficient. The general was obviously shocked at anyone daring to criticize the higher Party authorities.

We decided to wait. Erica was not well and, though we wanted to get her to proper medical treatment as soon as possible, we felt that rest in peaceful surroundings would be better than continual travel. We were put up at a hostel for travellers. Hsiao Li and I were quite happy there and it gave us the opportunity to look round. However, our boy, Sung Wei-ming, and Erica's nurse felt that people of our status should really have been put up at headquarters; two days later General Hsiao K'e arrived and we were invited to move there. We were asked with Hsiao K'e to the performance of a classical opera in which the hero was a man who tried to assassinate Ch'in Shih Huang Ti, the emperor who unified China in 221 B.C. and who has been notorious in Chinese history as an oppressive tyrant. We later saw another performance of this opera at Yenan; and it is interesting that, since the start of the campaign against Confucius in 1973, the Communists have treated Ch'in Shih Huang Ti as a hero.

Another lorry did arrive about a week later and we were among a fairly large party that got on for the return journey to Yenan, which still took nearly a week because it rained. Several times the lorry got stuck in deep mud and teams had to be mobilised from the nearest village to pull it out. Finally, the driver decided to wait until the road had dried. Though this was the time of year before winter wheat had been harvested, when food is most scarce, we found that people in the villages were still eating wheat and, in one village, I saw a man feeding corn to pigs.

U.S. plane circling to land at Yenan.

Suiteh to Yenan. Lorry being pulled out of mud.

Yenan, May 1944 — November 1945.

Although it was late May there was little sign of spring in Yenan. We could see that the city wall had been severely bombed and inside it was in ruins. Chin Ch'eng, the manager of our guest house, showed us round. A courtyard just inside the gate had been turned into a baseball ground, there was a large and comfortable dining hall and reception hall and in the distance the tiers and tiers of caves cut out of the yellow hillside — the traditional Yenan dwellings. Two of these were soon to be our living quarters. Each was about ten feet by twenty or twenty five and ten feet high in the middle, the front nearly all door or window with paper pasted on a wooden frame and there was a large desk and several chairs, all highly polished. Mr. Chin told us with pride that these were locally made and the polish stain resistant.

We were asked to meet Mao Tse-tung and Chu Te at a magnificent feast of the local wine and pork, chicken and beef cooked a variety of ways. When talking with Mao he said that whatever my reasons for coming to China it was very fortunate for them to have my help in defeating the Japanese and that they were very grateful for my efforts and touched by the way in which we had endured the hard life with them. When I asked what I could do at Yenan he told me to rest some more and we would talk of this another time. Later Mao invited us to drive with him to a lecture he was to give to the cadres of the Party School; his car was an ambulance that had been presented by the South Seas Overseas Chinese.

We got to know Yeh Chien-ying, Lin Piao, P'eng Te'huai and other leaders; the only people who were not friendly were Liu Shao-ch'i, P'eng Chen and Kao Kang. We met at formal parties but received the impression that they did not wish for contact with anyone not in the Party.

With nothing to do I became restless and asked Mr. Chin to discuss the matter with someone and so we were invited to lunch at Wang Chia P'ing with General Chu Te and the Division Commander, Lin Piao and his wife, Yeh Ch'un. After lunch we inspected Chu Te's private vegetable garden; Yenan was working to increase production and everyone was trying to become more self-sufficient. It was said that Mao Tse-tung had learnt spinning and that Chu Te was an excellent gardener. General Yeh Chien-yeng told us that his lettuces were the finest in Yenan, even better than those on the Border Region government's experimental farm. Chu Te and I then went to his study to discuss my work and I was appointed technical adviser to the Eighteenth Group Army communications department. (I still have my commission signed by Chu Te.) The department was in a small valley about ten miles from Yenan and their resources were much better than in Chin-Ch'a-Chi. Power supplies came from several old truck engines running off producer gas from charcoal.

I worked out that the power supply and transmitting valves available would allow us to build a transmitter giving about six hundred watts and thought this would be enough to reach the United States if we built a good directional aerial. Luckily I had copied down a number of formulae from the copy of Terman's *Radio Engineering* we had finally acquired in Chin-Ch'a-Chi and could design a V or rhombic aerial.

The leaders at Yenan were rather sceptical about my suggestion because the communications department had told them that they would be unable to make a transmitter which could be received abroad. However, they agreed that I should be allowed to try. Construction of the transmitter went smoothly but I had some trouble with the aerial. The chief technician of the communications department looked at a Mercator's projection map of the world and argued that San Francisco was almost due east from Yenan so the aerial should face down the valley. I managed to find a book on spherical trigonometry and worked out that the great circle bearing of San Francisco was somewhat north of northeast so the aerial should go across the valley. I got my way and it was agreed to put the transmitter on one hilltop with a big V going right across the valley. I also found a theodolite I could borrow, and went up one night to the site of the transmitter to get a sighting on the pole star and, the next morning, was able to direct the placing of the posts for the other ends of the aerial. When our transmissions started in August they could be received in San Francisco and the opposite side of the beam could be received in India.

Soon after our arrival at Yenan Chou En-lai came from Chungking and brought with him the first letters I had received from my parents since 1941; and a bit later the isolation of the Communist areas was broken by the arrival of a party of foreign correspondents. American Ambassador Gauss suggests in one of his dispatches that the National Government may have changed its policy of keeping the Communist areas isolated because of a belief in its own propaganda, a belief that, if the request of foreign correspondents to visit the Communist areas were granted, and if they stayed for some time in these areas, they would be disillusioned and produce highly unfavourable reports confirming the charges made in the National Government publicity. There is some confirmation of this hypothesis from the briefing given to the correspondents at Hu Tsung-nan's Headquarters in Sian. They were told that they would find large areas sown to opium poppy. In fact, they saw none. They were given a list of people executed by the Communists. In fact, they were able to interview many of them at Yenan. They were told that the Communists had not fought the Japanese since 1939; and so on. If the staff of Hu Tsung-nan's Headquarters knew that the charges against the Communists were false it would have been incredibly stupid to make them to journalists who would shortly be in a position to check them. However, if they genuinely believed them, it would have been sensible to tell the correspondents about things which they could try to check and which would descredit the Communists. The

Mao Tse-tung.

Chu Te.

Yeh Chien-ying.

Lin Piao.

Peng Te-huai.

Liu Shao-ch'i.

Chou En-lai.

Ho Lung.

correspondents' visit kept Hsiao Li very busy. She acted as one of the interpreters and often travelled round with Chou En-lai. At this time the Communists welcomed foreign observers and gave them every facility; some were allowed to travel to the front line areas in Shansi-Suiyuan.

The next excitement was the arrival of the U.S. Army Observers Section in July. To begin with Chinese Communist-U.S. relations were very friendly and the Communists began preparations for large scale co-operation. A school was started to train interpreters at which Hsiao Li taught some classes.

I was busy working with the Americans on plans for a communications network to transmit back to Yenan the information they wanted for the front line areas. They offered to provide equipment for a network of stations in the front line base areas whose primary use would be American though any spare capacity could be used by us. They asked us to handle their traffic on our network until their equipment was delivered; this seemed reasonable and we agreed, though most of our stations were very busy. The only ready-made American sets which would have been any good were those designed by OSS for use by the underground in occupied Europe, and even these were not entirely convenient when power came from a hand generator and not electric mains supply. We asked the Americans to supply hand generators, batteries and the components from which we could easily build really suitable sets.

I have published a long article on the development of Chinese Communist-U.S. relations in *Asia Quarterly* (Brussels, 1971, No. 3). To summarize, relations deteriorated after Ambassador General Patrick Hurley visited Yenan in early November 1944. General Hurley helped to work out a set of proposals for a Communist-Kuomintang settlement. He actually drafted some of the articles and, before leaving, signed the proposed terms saying that, though he could not commit his government, he was signing to show his personal support for the terms which were eminently fair and just. These gave the Communists almost everything they had been asking for — a coalition government and high command, recognition of all armies fighting the Japanese, and fair shares of American supplies for all armies. However, when, not surprisingly, these terms were rejected by the National Government, Hurley pressed the Communists to submit completely to the Nationalists. As a means of bringing pressure to bear he vetoed all proposals for co-operation with the Communists against the Japanese regardless of how much such co-operation could have helped the general allied war effort.

When Chou En-lai reported on the negotiations to one meeting at Yenan he asked rhetorically how one could deal with a government whose ambassador pledged his word and put his signature to it and then repudiated his promises a few weeks later. This was a fully justified complaint and General Hurley's policy produced many more detailed cases of American bad faith. The Americans would produce schemes for co-operation against the Japanese which involved quite large commitments of scarce Communist resources, such as the construction of several air fields in the front line base areas, and then the American contribution needed to make the scheme effective would be withheld.

In my own work, the Americans continued to want information from the front line areas but the promised equipment for their proposed communications network was never delivered. In late May 1945, the Americans delivered two plane loads of sets of a type we had told them was completely useless for the front line areas and which did not even yield very useful components if taken to bits. More than half the weight was a converter, weighing over seventy pounds, for getting power from a car battery though the Eighteenth Group Army had very few motor vehicles.

The Communist reaction to all this was rather stupid. They showed their dissatisfaction with the Americans by practically boycotting the Observers Section at Yenan and made public statements abusing General Hurley in rather vague terms, but they would never take a stand on particular issues where they were clearly in the right. I tried in vain to persuade General Yeh Chien-ying, the chief of staff, to give the Americans an ultimatum about the delivery of communications supplies saying that, unless the promised supplies were delivered within, say, another two months, American messages would go to lowest priority on our network. After the war Americans who had been in China told me that such an ultimatum would almost certainly have been effective. The Air Force alone, if threatened with the loss of weather reports from large areas of China, would have insisted that the promised equipment be delivered no matter how much Ambassador Hurley objected. Again, when rescued American airmen reached Yenan we at first broadcast their rescue on our news service. The Americans objected and said that they had a rule that such rescues should be given no publicity. This rule made sense when rescues were undertaken by an underground organisation in occupied territory. It made no sense at all for the Communist areas of China where the Japanese had known for years that uniformed Chinese troops were opposing them. The Communists suspected that the real reason for the American request was to prevent favourable publicity for them in America but, instead of ignoring it, they accepted it and grumbled.

A more important case is their treatment of General Hurley. Right up to his resignation in November 1945, Hurley continued to report to Washington that he was an acceptable mediator to both sides in China and was making progress in securing a

Kuomintang-Communist settlement. Suppose that, instead of vague abuse, the Communists had published their evidence of his bad faith and had declared that they could not accept his continued participation in negotiations with the National Government because they had good reason for distrusting his impartiality and his honesty. His position in China would then have become impossible and he would almost certainly have been recalled and perhaps replaced by someone who could have secured a peaceful settlement — which the Communists, at this time, said very emphatically was what they wanted. General Hurley was bitterly opposed by nearly all the China experts in the State Department.

This reliance on vague abuse rather than reasoned argument seemed to be an implication of the doctrinaire Communist point of view. I had one long argument on the subject with Ch'en Chia-k'ang and Huang Hua who were then the liaison officers with the Observers Section. Ch'en Po-ta had published a series of articles in the *Chieh Fang Jih Pao* (the Yenan paper) denouncing Yen Hsi-shan for collaboration with the Japanese but giving no evidence to support his abuse. I asked people whether there was any evidence and finally met a man who had been liaison officer with Yen Hsi-shan and was still in charge of Yen Hsi-shan affairs. He said that he had plenty of evidence and came round one evening with documents captured both from the Japanese and from Yen Hsi-shan's forces and a captured Yen Hsi-shan officer who told a very convincing story. (Hsiao Li could check that he was genuine and knew some of her father's former colleagues.) The next day at the Observers Section I remarked to Ch'en Chia-k'ang and Huang Hua that it seemed very silly to publish purely abusive articles when there existed good evidence to support the accusations they made. They were determined to defend the Party authorities and took the line that only Communists who understood dialectical materialism could believe something because of evidence. Other people's beliefs were determined by their class status so that all publicity could do was make people feel more strongly about their already determined beliefs. It was, therefore, pointless to set out evidence in newspaper articles.

The Americans, for different reasons, failed to press their most serious contention with the Communists. The behaviour of Communist Parties in Europe led them to suspect that the Chinese Communist Party might also be blindly subservient to the Soviet Union. High ranking officials wrote memoranda arguing that it would be contrary to American interests to allow Communist control of North China since this would merely replace a Japanese controlled puppet state with a Soviet one. The only official who seems to have taken a reasonable position was John Paton Davies who, unlike John Service, realised that relations between the Chinese Communists and the Soviet Union were a crucial question but he argued that it was not certain that the Chinese Communists would behave in the same way as European Communists and that it was important for the United States to find out.

If U.S. policy had followed Davies's advice the course of Chinese history might have developed along quite different lines. Properly handled, by either the Americans or the National Government, the issue of Soviet behaviour in Manchuria could have presented the Communists with a clear cut choice between Chinese patriotism and loyalty to the Soviet Union under Stalin. The Russians looted Manchurian industry under the pretext of "war booty", destroying the large scale heavy industry which the Chinese had expected to take over as the foundation for their post-war development. The discipline of Soviet troops towards the civilian population was also very bad with widespread looting and rape.

If the Communists had been forced to choose between Chinese patriotism and loyalty to Stalin the most likely result would have been a split in the Party with a few doctrinaire leaders going pro-Soviet but with the majority, including the army leaders, going pro-Chinese. A Communist party that had broken with the Soviet Union in 1946, instead of the 1960's, and with Stalin instead of with Krushchev, would have developed into something totally different from the present Chinese Communist Party.

Returning to life at Yenan, we lived in an official guest house. While at Suiteh, Erica's nurse had fallen in love with the leader of an army drama troupe and wished to stay with him, and though Hsiao Li was told that the nurse could be ordered to go on with us, she had no desire to compel her. Once at Yenan we found that, as we had been warned, it was impossible to get another nurse and Hsiao Li decided to ask one of the men who had looked after our baggage mules if he would take the job. At first he was reluctant saying he knew nothing about children but finally agreed and proved to be an excellent nurse. He became devoted to Erica and she to him. Lung Ku was an old Red Army man and had been with Mao Tse-tung's party on the Long March. He sympathized with Mao's decision to divorce his former wife and to marry Chiang Ch'ing because he had found the former Mrs. Mao to be a rather unpleasant woman, rude to subordinates and inclined to order even Mao himself around. Most of the survivors of the Long March had risen to high positions in the army but Lung Ku explained that he only wanted security and did not like responsibility. Several attempts had been made to promote him but he always deliberately made mistakes to get sent back to the ranks.

Po Ku (Chin Pang-hsien), head of New China News Agency.

Office of New China News Agency English language service.

Once our transmitter was working I became adviser to the English Language Service of the New China News Agency. I had two colleagues, Shen Chien-t'u and Ch'en Shu; our office was one of the Yenan caves and we had two old German typewriters with the z and the y transposed from the ordinary keyboard. We would get the Yenan paper in the morning and decide what was worth translating, sometimes consulting Po Ku, the head of the News Agency, and our translation had to be ready by four in the afternoon when a courier came to take it to the communications department. I did a certain amount of editing and got Po Ku to agree that the Chinese habit of continually applying abusive terms to political opponents was counter-productive for overseas publicity, and that good arguments against the Kuomintang were more effective as simple statements. On one occasion when I was ill and away from the office for a week or so, Shen Chien-t'u and Ch'en Shu did not have the courage to continue editing the official Party newspaper and I later saw an article in an American magazine saying that the Communist line in the negotiations must have changed because the Yenan news service had suddenly become much more abusive towards the Kuomintang.

Once at the news service I had much less to do with the communications department, partly because I was too busy and partly because they usually resented rather than welcomed my advice and I did not like their style of work. I found that they were allowing troops to leave for the front line with clumsy and obsolete equipment, and where in Chin-Ch'a-Chi we would have been ready to work sixteen hours a day to make sure that troops were going into combat with the best possible equipment, the department at Yenan was not prepared to change its routine to meet an emergency.

While material conditions were much more comfortable there, the general spirit of the organisation was less pleasant than in Chin-Ch'a-Chi. This was not just my impression. Other people coming from the front line areas would complain in private about the completely unnecessary bureaucracy and red tape they encountered. Long afterwards a former member of the Observers Section told me that even high ranking officers from the front line regions complained to him about the unpleasant atmosphere of intrigue and suspicion that they found at Yenan.

It was recognized that organisation at Yenan was often inefficient but the standard excuse was that Shensi-Kansu-Ninghsia was a poor and backward area. This possibly explained the behaviour of the local inhabitants but not the behaviour of people who had come from the most advanced areas of China. I used to tease them about this, saying that they seemed to believe incompetence was an infectious disease which anyone coming to Yenan was bound to catch. I diagnosed the trouble as lack of competition, provided in the front line areas by the Japanese, and even more to the greater dominance of the Party organisation. Party discipline inhibited criticism of anything that seemed to be backed by the Party although, in fact, the Party leaders were quite willing to accept criticism.

For instance, when we arrived at Yenan there was no standard time. Some organisations kept East China standard time, others Central China standard time, while the civilian government used the sundial in their courtyard, causing obvious confusion. Some months later the Central Committee issued a notice in the *Chieh Fang Jih Pao* that Yenan standard time should be based on the sundial, on the grounds that this was keeping close to the masses (Chinese peasants did not have sundials and had no need for greater accuracy than knowing the time to within an hour or so.) People privately complained of the impossibility of this decision as they had to keep schedules with stations in other parts of China, and sundial time is not even a constant difference from standard time. However, because the decision had come from the Central Committee no one protested openly. I had no such inhibition and wrote a letter to Mao Tse-tung pointing out that the civilized world had decided on a system of standard time zones and as far as I knew, the only person to put an area on local time had been Yen Hsi-shan who put Shansi province on T'aiyuan time, and surely the Communist Party did not wish to imitate a warlord, I then pointed out the practical inconvenience of sundial time. As a result Mao Tse-tung asked one of his secretaries to telephone round to all the organisations in Yenan asking what standard time would be convenient. A new notice then appeared in the *Chieh Fang Jih Pao* putting Yenan on Central China standard time, the time zone in which it belonged — and Mao Tse-tung sent me a letter thanking me for my criticism.

Again, when the visiting correspondents were taken to see the medical school they found that, because of a directive about self-sufficiency, the students were spending half their time farming. On their return they were asked if they had any criticisms and said that, if training medical personnel was really top priority, it would be reasonable to allot enough resources to the medical school to enable the students to spend most of their time on study. Apparently, no one from the medical school had ever dared to use this argument. While I was at Yenan I wrote a long report of forty or fifty single spaced pages entitled "What is wrong with Yenan" and gave copies to several of the Party leaders.

Our second child, James, was born at the end of January 1945 in the Bethune International Hospital. When Hsiao Li got back, the Interpreters' school had been closed because of worsening Communist — U.S. relations, and so she began teaching Chinese to some of the non-commissioned officers from the Observers Section who had almost nothing to do.

Over the next month or so Party leaders were moving to Yenan from all over the Communist areas for the forthcoming Seventh Party Congress. We met a number of old friends from Chin-Ch'a-Chi. The general atmosphere was optimistic because of the progress of the war. The News Agency monitored several foreign news services and we could see the German collapse coming through the increasingly erratic Transocean newscasts. In North China the Japanese were pulling back towards the railways and the Communists were starting to capture even the largest cities on the North China plain.

The proceedings of the Party Congress were effectively kept secret but certain key speeches were published. The Communist line at this time was asking for a coalition government and they were promising the Chinese people civil liberties and freedom of speech and publication.

Negotiations with the National Government had effectively broken down by April and, after the Congress, the Communists began preparing to set up their own "Liberated Areas" government. If the Japanese surrender had come a few months later there would have been two rival governments in China.

Meeting to celebrate V-J Day, Yenan.

The Japanese surrender produced a few days of enthusiasm but this was soon dampened by fears of civil war. At first the Japanese started to pull back to their main bases and a Communist takeover in North China was resisted only by the Chinese troops in Japanese service who now proclaimed their allegiance to the National Government but were not able to resist the Communist advance. After a week or so the Japanese started fighting again.

Towards the end of August, General Hurley invited Mao Tse-tung to come to Chungking for negotiations. There was some disagreement about whether he should accept the invitation and, asked for my opinion, I said that it would look rather bad abroad if Mao Tse-tung simply refused to talk though he could very well take a firm line once he got to Chungking.

left, Mao Tse-tung; middle, General Patrick Hurley, U.S. Ambassador to China 1944 — November 1945. Photo: U.S. Army Signal Corps.

General Hurley came to Yenan to escort Mao Tse-tung and I had the opportunity to talk to him. Hurley despised the Chinese. He asked whether I did not agree that they were hopeless people who must have a strong man on top to keep them in order. He also showed complete comtempt for the judgment of the American experts and had quite uncritically accepted all the charges made against the Communists by Kuomintang publicity.

Negotiations went on till the beginning of October and produced a lull in the civil war. People hoped for a peaceful settlement and though they believed a civil war might go on for ten years or more were fairly confident that the Communists could win in the end. They argued that it had taken the National Government a long time to defeat the Chinese Soviet Republic and that their relative strength was far greater than in the early 1930's. They also argued that the Japanese had never been able to eliminate the Communists in North China though they had been able to defeat the National Government armies whenever they chose to make a serious effort.

The negotiations produced a joint statement dated October 10th. which simply recorded an agreement to differ on nearly all practical issues and within ten days heavy fighting started when National Government troops tried advancing along the Peking-Hankow railway from Chengchow towards Shih-chia-chuang. Chou En-lai took this as a sign that the National Government was determined on war. He told us that, apart from the published agreement, the Communists had said that they would not oppose

National Government occupation of areas actually held by the Japanese but would fight if National Government forces tried to take over areas held by the Communists.

Another friend in the Party told us of a high level meeting after Mao had returned from Chungking when he was criticized for having made real concessions, such as withdrawing from south of the Yangtze, in exchange for nothing but vague promises. His critics argued that he should have known that reactionaries could not be trusted and would never yield except to force. In the end Mao won a vote of confidence by arguing that civil war would be so harmful to the Chinese people that it was worth taking considerable risks in the hope of avoiding it.

Lindsay family at Yenan.

Erica, Hsiao Li, James, Yenan.

Hsiao Li spinning, Yenan.

Return to England via Chungking, November 1945.

General Nieh Jung-chen had asked me to return to Chin-Ch'a-Chi to help in setting up a new administration for Kalgan, one of the few large cities the Communists had taken over. If conditions had been peaceful this would have been a very interesting job but, with two small children, I had no wish to become involved in a long period of civil war.

We therefore decided to return to England. We had one long farewell talk with Mao Tse-tung who reiterated his hopes that there could be a peaceful settlement. Chiang Ch'ing was also present but said nothing. During all this time at Yenan she had kept completely out of politics and though Hsiao Li often had long conversations with her at parties Chiang Ch'ing kept these purely personal and never even discussed the progress of the war.

The Observers Section flew us to Chungking which had been largely rebuilt since 1940. We soon decided that primitive arrangements which worked were better than modern conveniences which did not. At Yenan we had only paraffin lamps but there was ample oil from the local oil wells. At Chungking there was electric light but the voltage was so low the filament only glowed a dull red. At Yenan there was no running water but, when we wanted to give the children a bath, there were people to draw water from the well, heat it in the kitchen and bring it in a bucket to our cave. In Chungking there was a bath with hot and cold taps but no water came out.

Hsiao Li was very pleased to meet her brother who was working with the Bank of China. My rather poor impression of British officialdom was confirmed. The Australians and the Canadians were keenly interested to learn everything about the situation in the Communist areas and we had long talks with them. In the British Embassy the only people who showed the slightest interest

Lung Ku with Erica and James, Yenan.

were Colonel Harmon of military intelligence and a former businessman on a temporary appointment. The ambassador gave us a formal dinner but was careful also to invite a National Government official and made no attempt to get information from us. We did have one short talk with General Carton de Wiart, who had been sent to China as Churchill's personal representative, but what we said can have made no impression because he later wrote a book in which he stated that, throughout the war, the Communists had controlled a continuous area in Northwest China.

Colonel Harmon's experience showed us how far the Americans had tried to monopolize contacts with the Communists. When the Observers Section arrived in Yenan, Colonel Barrett had brought a letter to me from Harmon saying that he would like to visit Yenan and asking me to find out if he would be welcome. I mentioned this to General Yeh Chien-ying who said that he would certainly be welcome, adding that, if the Americans were not passing on all the information they were getting at Yenan, he would be glad to give me copies to send to Colonel Harmon. I reported this in a letter that Colonel Barrett took when he went back to Chungking and had been puzzled not to receive any further communication from Colonel Harmon. In Chungking we learned that he had never received my letter. Presumably the Americans at Chungking had surpressed it. He had made repeated attempts to get to Yenan but the Americans always said that their planes were overloaded, though they often had room for an American correspondent. Finally, he was called in to see the ambassador and found Sir Horace Seymour with General Hurley who at once said that he had heard that Colonel Harmon had gone to Yenan against his orders. Sir Horace did not ask General Hurley why the American Ambassador should claim the right to give orders to a British officer in China, he only mumbled

something unintelligible and Colonel Harmon was forced to explain that he had never managed to get to Yenan.

We spent about ten days at Chungking before taking a plane to Calcutta, where we were afraid that we might be stuck for several months and could only find a rather uncomfortable small hotel. However, I met a newspaper editor who suggested I try the organisation for Returned Allied Prisoners of War and Internees. I explained to them that we had not been prisoners or internees but had spent nearly two and a half years in a guerilla area behind the Japanese lines. On the strength of this they took us in, transported us to the old viceroy's palace which was comfortable though crowded and, within a week, flew us back to England.

We arrived at Poole by flying boat after night stops at Karachi, Alexandria and Sicily; spent a few hours with my aunts in London and reached my parents at Oxford that evening. Some of our luggage was stolen on the train, my first experience of post-war England.

Lindsay family at Master's Lodging, Balliol College.

Historical Analysis

Soviet analysts of Chinese Communism now maintain that the Chinese Communists started to deviate from Marxist-Leninist orthodoxy during the war against Japan. From a very different standpoint, they agree with the view given in this book.

Though Chinese Communist historians now try to deny it, there is clear evidence that the main lines of Chinese Communist policy were decided by the Comintern up to the mid-1930's. Comintern directives were not so stupid as some Western writers have tried to make out; they were actually ahead of the Chinese Communist leadership in advocating a revolution based on the peasants. However, though Marxist-Leninist theory often gives quite good guidance about how to win power, it offers very poor guidance about how to use power when it has been won. Before 1936, the Chinese Communists in the areas they controlled insisted on the universality of class warfare and tried to fit Chinese rural society into categories worked out by Lenin for pre-revolutionary Russia. They obtained strong support from the landless labourers and poorer tenant farmers who shared land confiscated from class enemies, but landlords and rich peasants were treated as irreconcilable enemies while frequent changes in the regulations for dividing friend and enemy made the position of middle peasants insecure. There was no incentive to be an efficient farmer when the result might be classification as a class enemy.

Policies started to change in 1936 and, with the United Front agreement of September 1937, the Communists gave up their specifically Communist policies. This put them in a position to follow policies that really did benefit the people and won them almost universal popular support. While landlords lost something, they knew that they would be much worse off under Japanese control; and were also patriotic Chinese. Because there was no important discrepancy between what the Communists were doing and what they claimed to be doing, they were not afraid of thinking clearly, of engaging in reasoned discussion, or of observation by visitors from outside. Both in Chin-Ch'a-Chi and in Shensi-Kansu-Ninghsia we could see that the moderate reasonable policies of this period had really improved the conditions of the peasants and had markedly increased productivity where damage by the Japanese was not too serious.

One can deduce with a fair amount of confidence what would have happened if the Communists had continued to follow their war-time policies. There would have been more rapid economic progress and a great deal more freedom. It follows that the later policies of liquidating landlords, collectivization, and the formation of communes were quite unnecessary as a means for giving the Chinese people enough to eat. They only make sense as the implementation of Marxist-Leninist-Maoist dogma and as means for bringing the people firmly under the control of the Communist Party.

Actually, when General Marshall failed to be an impartial mediator and the truce agreement started to break down in the spring of 1946, the Communists turned for support to the Soviet Union and swung back towards Marxist-Leninist orthodoxy, returning to their pre-1936 agrarian policies. By 1948, even their own publications admitted that this had alienated a large proportion of the middle peasants. By 1949, Mao Tse-tung was saying that the Chinese must take the Communist Party of the Soviet Union as their teachers and the Soviet Union as their model.

A generalisation that explains a great deal about developments in the People's Republic of China is that the Communists have done a good job, wherever their Marxist-Leninist theory is irrelevant. So far as I know there is nothing in the works of Marx, Engels, Lenin, Stalin or Mao about how to organise a public health service, how to extend irrigation and flood control, how to improve communications, how to expand electrification into the countryside, and so on. In such fields the Communists have been willing to use common sense, to take the advice of technical experts and have provided drive and organising ability with very good results. Where Marxist-Leninist doctrine applies, common sense vanishes.

In the late 1950's the Chinese Communists again started to diverge from Soviet orthodoxy, but in the opposite direction. Instead of returning to the reasonable scientific spirit of the war-time period they became Marxist-Leninist fundamentalists. While they denounce the Soviet Union they continue to praise Stalin

The British Labour Party's visit to the People's Republic of China. A group taken on the steps of the Peace Hotel, Peking. Our group shows, left to right, front row, Mr. W. Burke, Chairman of the Labour Party; Mr. Aneurin Bevin, M.P., Mr. Clement Attlee, M.P., leader of the delegation; Mr. Chou En-lai, Chinese Premier and Foreign Minister; Dr. Edith Summerskill, M.P., Vice-President of the Labour Party, and Mr. H. Franklin. Second row: Lord Lindsay of Birker, interpreter; Mr. Morgan Phillips, Secretary of the Labour Party; Mr. Sam Watson, Mr. Harry Earnshaw and Mr. Chang Hsi-jo, head of the Chinese Institute of Foreign Affairs. The group includes other members of the Chinese Government; and Lady Lindsay, an interpreter daughter of Colonel Li Wen Chi. Mr. Chou En-lai has expressed hopes of friendlier Sino-British relations. Chinese characters read: "Presented to Mr. and Mrs. Michael Lindsay", signed and dated by Chou En-lai.

Mr. Attlee with Chinese interpreter. Hangchow.

even though the specific evils they denounce in the Soviet Union reached their high point under Stalin — acting as an imperialist power, using secret police terrorism against the masses, the Communist Party becoming a new privileged ruling class, and so on.

Essentially, in the People's Republic the Communist leaders are using the Chinese people as raw material with whom they try to build their ideal utopian society and whom they try to turn into their ideal type of men and women. The people may derive some incidental benefits from this but it is not really serving them.

Hsiao Li and I visited China in 1949, 1954 and 1973. There had been great material progress in the public sector and, perhaps, some levelling up of the lowest economic conditions. But the standard of clothing is not markedly better than that shown in the photographs of Chin-Ch'a-Chi and, though villages now have electric light, most houses in them are shabbier than those shown in the photographs from 1938 and 1939. On the non-material side there has been great deterioration, not only compared with the war-time period but also compared with 1949 and 1954. Recently there has been a systematic attempt to eliminate traditional Chinese culture and, in 1973, people told us that they no longer kept up long-standing close personal friendships because it was safest not to have any social contacts outside one's own immediate family.

When people accuse Hsiao Li and me of having changed our principles, — supporting the Communists in the 1940's and the Kuomintang in the 1970's, we reply that we have applied constant principles to changing organisations. During the war against Japan the Communists were really serving the Chinese people. Now the Chinese people are getting much better service from the Kuomintang. The superiority of Taiwan is not merely in a higher general standard of living, though this is very noticeable; there is also the survival and development of Chinese culture and the traditional Chinese way of life. The people in Taiwan enjoy a far greater degree of freedom than those under Communist rule. This is not just a matter of less regimentation and control, of their personal affairs, but extends to intellectual and even to political activity. As compared to North America and Western Europe, intellectual and political freedom in Taiwan is limited but still compares favourably with any other Asian country except Japan.

Glossary

Dr. Norman Bethune. Canadian surgeon. Member Canadian Communist Party. Worked in Spanish Civil War. Went to China at end of 1937 and worked in Chin-Ch'a-Chi from 1938 until his death from blood poisoning in 1939.

General Chang Yin-wu. Former minor warlord. Went back to Hopei with Lu Chung-lin in 1938 and attempted to re-assert control of his former area. Involved in fighting with Communists in 1939.

Ch'en Li-fu. Important political figure in right wing of Kuomintang. Retired to United States after 1949.

Chiang I-chen. Gave up medical work and, in the People's Republic, had a position connected with agriculture in the Fukien provincial government. At one time he got into trouble but was later appointed to a position in the Ministry of Agriculture in Peking.

chin Chinese unit of weight, about one and one third pounds.

Chin-Ch'a-Chi. All Chinese provinces have single character classical names as well as their usual two character names. Shansi-Ch'ahar-Hopei was always referred to as Chin-Ch'a-Chi (Chin being an old kingdom with approximately the same area as the modern Shansi province, Ch'a just the first syllable of Ch'a-ha-erh, a Mongol name, and Chi the name for another old kingdom roughly coinciding with modern Hopei). For convenience I follow the Chinese custom, using the shorter classical version, namely Chin-Ch'a-Chi.

General Chu Te. Born 1886. Graduate of Yunnan Officers School. Served under Ts'ai Ao in 1916 campaign against Yuan Shih-kai. Went to Europe in early 1920's. Took part in Nan-ch'ang revolt in 1927 which is now celebrated as birth of Red Army. Joined Mao Tse-tung at Ching-kang-shan in April 1928, and remained as leading Communist general. Still has honoured position in People's Republic.

General Hsiao K'e. During the civil war in the 1920's and early 1930's was with the Red Army under General Ho Lung in West Hunan. He got into trouble in 1959 because of association with General P'eng Te-huai but has been rehabilitated and holds position connected with army education.

hsien Chinese government area roughly equivalent to an English or American county. There are about two thousand *hsien* in China.

hsien-chang The official in charge of a hsien. Under the empire this was the lowest position filled by members of the regular civil service.

General Hsu Hsiang-chien. In late 1920's and early 1930's was Red Army Commander in Hopei-Anhui-Honan Region with Chang Kuo-t'ao. During war with Japan moved to Shantung in 1938 and became commander of Shantung Region. Still in favour in People's Republic.

k'ang The typical North China farmhouse had a platform with the flue running to and fro underneath the surface which could be heated in winter for sitting or sleeping. In superior houses the *k'ang* was fired from outside but the ordinary peasants' houses had a cauldron for cooking at the corner of the *k'ang* to combine cooking and heating. In summer the fire could be by-passed direct to the chimney. One could be comfortable on a *k'ang* even when room temperature was below freezing.

kao-liang is a variety of sorghum which grows about ten feet high and is a common crop in North China.

Kuomintang Nationalist Party, founded by Sun Yat-sen. Controlled government of China from 1927 to 1949. Now controls Taiwan.

Lo Chia-lun. At one time head of Peking University and gave Mao Tse-tung his job as library assistant. Worked in Taiwan supervising publication of Kuomintang archives.

General Lü Cheng-ts'ao. Officer in National 29th. Army. Remained in Central Hopei when 29th. Army retreated in 1937. Became Eighth Route Army Commander in Central Hopei until latter part of 1943 when he was transferred to command of Shansi-Suiyan Region. Elected candidate member of Communist Central Committee in 1945. Was Minister of Railways in People's Republic but was dismissed during Cultural Revolution for failing to provide enough transport for Red Guards.

General Lu Chung-lin. Former subordinate of Feng Yü-hsiang who went over to National Government in 1930. Appointed Governor of Hopei in 1938 but was forced to retire by Japanese offensive in 1939.

General Nieh Jung-chen. Native of Szechuan province. Went to Europe in 1920 on "work study" scheme and was one of the few students who actually worked (in an electrical factory), and studied (chemistry at a worker's college at Charleroi), instead of spending time on politics. Was with Red Army in South China and participated in Long March. At beginning of war with Japan was political commissar to 115th. Division under Lin Piao. When Lin Piao was wounded he became both commander and political commissar of Chin-Ch'a-Chi. In 1949 was Mayor of Peking. Later Chief of Staff during Korean War. Since then has concentrated on technical work and has been in charge of Chinese atomic weapons programme.

General P'eng Te-huai. Chu Te's deputy in command of Eighth Route (later called Eighteenth Group) Army during war against Japan. Became Minister of Defence in People's Republic but was purged in 1959 for opposing Mao Tse-tung's policies of communes and the "Great Leap Forward".

Sun Yat-sen. Born in Kuangtang province in 1856. Educated at missionary school in Hawaii and took Western medical training at Hongkong. Started revolutionary activities in 1890's. Founder of Kuomintang. Elected provisional president of the Republic of China in 1911. Led rival government of Republic of China in Canton from 1917 on. Accepted Soviet aid and alliance with Communists in 1923 after failure to obtain support from Western powers. Died 1925. His political works are far sighted and show great insight in general principles but are often badly confused in details. Still accepted as political authority by the Kuomintang on Taiwan.

Wang Ching-wei. Became famous as revolutionary through attempt to assassinate Manchu Prince Regent, was not executed because of his beautiful calligraphy. Became close associate of Sun Yat-sen and was Chiang Kai-shek's rival in Kuomintang politics after Sun Yat-sen's death in 1925. At end of 1938 went from Chungking to French Indo-China and started negotiations with Japanese which ended with Wang Ching-wei starting Japanese sponsored government at Nanking in March 1940. Died before end of the war.

Professor Wu Wen-tsao. Professor of Sociology at Yenching University. Moved to Union University, Yunnan in 1938. Now working in Minority Races Research Institute at Peking.

General Yen Hsi-shan. Native of Wu-t'ai *hsien*, Shansi. Graduate of Pao-ting Officers School and Japanese Officers Training School, fellow student with Chiang Kai-shek. Appointed Governor of Shansi Province by Yuan Shih-kai in 1912 and remained in control of province, except for short intervals, until 1949.

Chronology

1911. Revolution against Manchu dynasty. Sun Yat-sen becomes Provisional President of the Republic.

1912. Manchu dynasty abdicates. Yuan Shih-k'ai becomes President of the Republic of China.

1913. Sun Yat-sen's supporters revolt unsuccessfully against Yuan-Shih-k'ai.

1916. Yuan Shih-k'ai proclaims himself a new emperor, faces revolt and withdraws as emperor and dies soon afterwards. Period of civil wars between rival warlords starts.

1917. Sun Yat-sen becomes president of rival government in Canton.

1921. July. Founding of Chinese Communist Party.

1923. Sun Yat-sen, having failed to get support from Western powers and having been driven from Canton by Ch'en Chiung-ming, reaches agreement with Comintern representative Adolf Joffe to receive Soviet aid and to allow Chinese Communist members also to become Kuomintang party members.

1925. Sun Yat-sen dies.

1926. Start of Northern Expedition. Kuomintang and Communist alliance starts campaign from Kuangtung to conquer rest of China.

1927. After fall of Shanghai in April, Chiang Kai-shek breaks with the Communists.

1928. New National Government of China established by Kuomintang. Continuation of Northern Expedition captures Peking and gets control of China south of Great Wall.

Chu Te and Mao Tse-tung join up at Ching-kang-shan and start serious development of Communist insurgency in south China countryside.

1929. Various civil wars between National Government and warlords. Spread of Communist insurgency. Chang Hsueh-liang, the Manchurian warlord states his allegiance to National Government.

1931. Japanese start conquest of Manchuria, with the Mukden incident. In November the Communists proclaim formation of Chinese Soviet Republic.

1932. Japanese declare establishment of Manchoukuo under former Chinese emperor.

1934. New National Government fort and blockade line strategy against Communist bases in South China forces the Communists to retire in Long March.

1935. Ho-Umetsu Agreement gives Japanese increased influence in North China. Developing anti-Japanese movement among Chinese students.

1936. First groups of Red Army arrive in North Shensi to join up with local Communist insurgency. Communists call for united front against Japan and reach agreement with Chang Hsueh-liang whose troops are supposed to be fighting them. December, Sian Incident. Chiang Kai-shek goes to Sian to secure continuation of war against Communists, is seized by Chang Hsueh-liang. Chou En-lai acts as mediator and secures Chiang Kai-shek's release and civil war effectively ends.

1937. July 7th. Start of Sino-Japanese war with fighting near Peking (Lu-k'ou-ch'iao Incident). Latter part of August, war becomes general. Shanghai falls in December and National Government retires from Nanking to Wuhan. In September Communists and National Government reach formal agreement for united front. Communist forces in North China recognised as 8th. Route Army, later 18th. Group Army, with three divisions and Communist remnants in South China recognised as New 4th. Army.

1938. September. Japanese capture Canton and Wuhan. National Government retires to Chungking. October, Japanese start serious attempts to get control of countryside in North China.

1939. National Government defeats Japanese attempt to capture Ch'angsha and front between National Government and Japanese remains fairly stable until 1944. United front starts to break down with first full scale fighting between regular National Government and Communist units in the winter of 1939-40. War in Europe starts in September.

1940. March. Wang Ching-wei, Chiang Kai-shek's rival in the Kuomintang, sets up new Japanese sponsored government in Nanking. Japanese try to bring pressure on National Government by heavy bombing of Chungking.

In North China, Japanese start fort and blockade line strategy against Communist areas. In August, Communists stage the Hundred Regiment Campaign.

1941. December. Outbreak of war between Japan and the U.S. and Britain. Japanese capture Hongkong and start invasion of Malaya.

1942. Japanese conquest of Burma cuts China off from land communication with Allies. The "Hump" airlift is started to get supplies from India to China but is on a very small scale at first. Americans start air bases in South China which become increasingly successful in operations against Japanese shipping.

1943. Relations worsen between Communists and National Government. Japanese control in North China reaches a maximum.

1944. Japanese start campaigns to get complete control of Peking-Wuhan-Canton rail line and to eliminate American air bases in South China. Weakening of Japanese forces in North China starts accelerating loss of the countryside to the Communists.

Communist-Kuomintang negotiations start at Sian but produce no result. General Stilwell is recalled in September and replaced by General Wedemeyer. U.S. ambassador resigns and is replaced by General Hurley.

Contacts between Communist areas and the outside world start with visit of correspondent's party to Yenan in May and arrival of U.S. Army Observers Section in July.

1945. At Yalta Conference the U.S.S.R. agrees to join war against Japan three months after German surrender. In August use of first atom bombs and Soviet conquest of Manchuria lead to Japanese surrender.

Civil war in China starts soon after Japanese surrender. General Hurley resigns in November and, in December, General Marshall comes on special mission to China.

1946. General Marshall is at first successful in securing truce agreement but this starts to break down in April and events move towards renewed civil war.

1947. General Marshall resigns position in China in January and full scale civil war starts. At first the National Government is successful in extending area under its control but fails to eliminate Communist armies who have started to get Soviet aid in 1946.

1948. Course of civil war turns sharply against the National Government.

1949. Communists win civil war though some operations in West China continue into 1950. National Government retires to Taiwan and Communists set up People's Republic of China on October 1st.

Bibliography

The Rise of Modern China. By Immanuel C. Y. Hsu. New York, Oxford University Press, 1970.
(This is probably the best general history of China from the mid-19 th. century on for accurate factual information.)

Peasant Nationalism and Communist Power. By Chalmers Johnson. Stanford University Press, 1967.
(This is the most complete history of the war between the Chinese Communists and the Japanese between 1937 and 1945. It is based mainly on Japanese sources.)

Red Star over China. By Edgar Snow. Penguin Books, 1972.
(Edgar Snow was the first foreign journalist to visit the Chinese Communists. He obtained lengthy interviews with the Chinese Communist leaders and give a good general picture of the Communist base in North Shensi in 1936. Some of the information they gave him about previous events was not accurate but, at the time, he had no way of checking this.)

The Yenan Way in Revolutionary China. By Mark Selden. Harvard University Press, 1972.
(This is a detailed study of the development and organisation of the Shensi-Kansu-Ninghsia Region and gives a good account of the Communist policies of the war time period. It somewhat exaggerates the importance of Shensi-Kansu-Ninghsia as compared to the other Communist regions.)

Mao Tse-tung. By Stuart Schram. Penguin Books, 1970.
(A good general biography of Mao Tse-tung.)

Chinese Communism in 1927. By Hsiao Tso-liang. Chinese University of Hongkong Press, 1970.
(This is a very good account of the split between the Communists and the Kuomintang and the start of the civil war which continued to 1937. It effectively disproves the myth that Mao Tse-tung was defying Comintern orthodoxy in basing the revolution on the peasants.)

Mao and China. By Stanley Karnow. Macmillan, 1973.
(Stanley Karnow was the most scholarly of the "China watcher" journalists in Hongkong and his book gives a good account of developments in the People's Republic of China.)

China Today. By Klaus Mehnert. Thames and Hudson, 1972.
(Klaus Mehnert is a German scholar who had made a number of visits to China.)